WRITING NON-FICTION THAT SELLS

THAT SELLS

By Jackie Sherman

Emerald Guides

© First Edition Jackie Sherman 2014

British Library Cataloguing in Publication Data. A catalogue record is available for this book from the British Library.

ISBN 978-1-84716-424-7

Printed and bound by The Grosvenor Group London

Cover design by Bookworks Islington

CONTENTS

CH. 1

INTRODUCTION

Unlike some forms of writing such as poetry or memoirs, where people often write as therapy or for self-fulfilment alone, most non-fiction material is written to be read by others. If you aren't published, it's frustrating and makes all your hard work seem pointless.

For success as a writer, you need to be sure:

- your writing fulfils a need, whether teaching new skills, entertaining your audience or providing valuable information
- you have analysed the market carefully
- your material is well organised and well written, making it a pleasure for readers to spend time on
- you target your submissions appropriately
- you write with an authoritative and original voice, so that you as the author and the knowledge or experience you are sharing are credible and will appear fresh and new to readers

This book will show you how to develop these skills and maximise the chances of selling your work.

There are a large number of writing guides on the subject of non-fiction in bookshops, but unlike many of those available, this book is not a theoretical work but is based on hard-won experience in the business of getting paid for writing. If you look on Amazon, you will see that I have published over 30 books with publishers such as Pearsons, Hodder Education, Age Concern, How To Books, Green Books, Emerald Publishing and Elsevier. My work has also appeared in a wide range of magazines and newspapers including Waterways World, The Times Educational Supplement, Yours, Canals & Rivers, Writers' Forum, Somerfield magazine, Olive, Computer Active, Edge magazine, Writing magazine, The New Writer, Freelance Market News and The Guardian. I write a regular monthly column, articles and book reviews for the website www.laterlife.com and have written course material for a number of distance learning colleges. I currently tutor a distance learning course on 'writing non-fiction'.

By sharing my experiences I hope that you too will succeed in getting your work published: whether occasional, one-off pieces or regular freelance contributions. To help you, I have designed a number of exercises that I hope you find time for. Mastering such skills as analysing markets, being original, identifying your strengths, planning content and editing your drafts is really the only way to achieve your aim of being successful in the world of non-fiction writing.

Just a note about the word "published." This is used as a generic term meaning any form of publication that can be read by others. The advice in this book relates just as much to writing that ends up as online content or ebooks as it does to the more common forms of hard copy and it is very important to stay flexible. In many cases, if something submitted to a print publication is rejected, you may find that it will be published online with hardly any changes, and there is an enormous amount of cross-over when it comes to writing for one medium or another.

WHAT IS NON-FICTION?

The range of subjects and potential approaches you can take with non-fiction are so vast that listing them here would be quite impossible. All you need bear in mind is that non-fiction is writing based on fact rather than coming solely from the imagination and it is usually written for a purpose such as entertaining, informing, inspiring or persuading.

Here are just a few examples of the non-fiction genre:

- A detailed or historical examination of anything from a single location to a business, fashion, philosophy, dynasty, literary genre, religion, job type or political system
- Biographies
- Autobiographies and memoirs
- Diaries, journals or letters relating feelings or experiences over time
- Scientific, psychological or environmental treaties
- Eye witness reports of events
- Essays, reflections, speeches or sermons
- History
- Travelogues and travel guides
- Instructional guides
- Celebrity gossip
- Encyclopaedias and dictionaries
- Textbooks and course materials
- Reviews
- Research findings
- Information or views expressed through interviews and questionnaire responses

TREATMENTS

Deciding on the best treatment for your subject matter can be tricky as there are many different ways to write about someone or something. If you take the example of Picasso, depending on your own background and access to documentation you might be able to produce an analysis of his art; write a biography; collate diary entries or letters that he wrote; describe a meeting you had with him; write travel pieces based around the places he lived and worked; include him in a book specifically for children about great painters of the 20th century; provide instructions on how to paint in his style; include an examination of his work in an art textbook; review an exhibition of his work or a book about his paintings; or interview people who knew him.

One of the joys of non-fiction is that there is always scope to write something unique in a style that suits you, whether or not others have already written about your chosen subject.

EXERCISE 1

1. *Taking your own town or village, brainstorm different ways you could write about it e.g. a travel guide or the history of one of the buildings. Don't worry at this stage whether it would be difficult or not or if you have the necessary knowledge or experience.*
2. *Are there any treatments that appeal to you more than others?*

REASONS FOR WRITING NON-FICTION

There are a number of different reasons why people set out to write non-fiction, and they include:

Personal feelings. Many letters, articles, blogs and books are written because the writer has something they want to say. It can be a comment, recommendation, accolade or jokey reply following a news report or something you have recently read or heard about, or it may be a very strongly held view, such as concern about the building of a new shopping centre; a disagreement with something a politician has announced; or a warning about a major issue like climate change. The only problem for writers in these cases is that if you do feel strongly you can get carried away, and no editor will publish an angry tirade or libellous material. You must always control your personal feelings and write in a reasoned and/or entertaining way as that is the most effective method for getting your point across and persuading others to agree with you.

Sharing an experience or expertise. After some months or even years becoming an expert, gaining knowledge and experience, following certain rules or making a discovery, it is common to want to write about these things so that you can share them with others. You may want to open people's eyes to something you have been working on or thinking about; provide them with new or enhanced skills; help them pass exams; or tell them about aspects of your life such as living in a care home or bringing up twins to entertain, inspire, warn or at least prepare them for a similar experience.

To be published: Very often, if you want to make money from writing you have to find something to write about that does not affect you personally. This is where analysing the market - what gets published and what people are reading - is crucial if you are to find suitable topics.

It doesn't matter which category your writing falls into, and often you can write for a combination of different reasons, but recognising what motivates you may be helpful when you decide what to write and where it should be targeted.

THE INSPIRATION FOR NON-FICTION WRITING

Non-fiction often comes about through a personal story or the expansion of an experience writers have had in real life. A travel piece written following an actual holiday or business trip; a letter recounting an amusing incident that took place in your corner shop; or an illustrated step-by-step guide to making a handbag are all common examples. In one sense they are relatively easy to write because the facts and figures are readily available. Equally common are books and articles still based on real life but developed from experience or knowledge gleaned over a longer time period. For example, someone may write a "running a restaurant" book after spending twenty years in the business; or an article detailing "ten ways to overcome arachnophobia" with advice based on their own attempts to find a solution.

In many cases, you may have an idea for a piece that goes into unknown territory. Although you are not able to draw on your own experience, you can still investigate and research the topic perfectly adequately. Bear in mind, though, that in those cases where you are analysing situations or offering advice, you do need to take care that your work is accurate and of an acceptable standard as experts in the field may well read and comment on it. The last thing you want to write is a "how to" book or article, for example, that clearly demonstrates you don't actually know how to yourself.

A foolproof way to cover something new without fear of getting it wrong is to interview people or use questionnaires to provide the answers, as the authenticity of the voices in your work will give it all the credibility you need.

EXAMPLE
An excellent book based almost entirely on interviews is "Earning money after you've retired" by Rosie Staal. She interviewed over 50 people from stone carvers to dog walkers, landladies and fitness instructors. She asked them all the same five questions: why are you still working, what are you doing, how did it come about, is it working out well and what about the money? Being able to compare the answers makes it easy for readers to understand what drove those featured and the pros and cons of their choices.

Finally, a different approach is to make use of material already published – either in magazines, books, archives or on various websites – and give it your own emphasis. Historical books (apart from your own memoirs) obviously fall into this category but there are many others that may do so such as books on bizarre adventurous sports, medical conditions, types of job, travel or gardening.

Works of this type may need to be created at least partly from other people's material simply because it would be impossible to carry out all the activities, treat all the illnesses, visit all the places or grow all the plants that you need to cover in your own publication, if you want it to be comprehensive.

IMPROVING THE CONTENT

Where your material is based on personal experience, it may be appropriate in some cases to consider widening its scope and appeal by adding further details of a more general nature. For example, if you write about a course you attended, you could add details of alternative courses readers might attend, or list directories they could use to find a course nearby. Again, if you describe an adventure that involved travelling by Eurostar before backpacking round Europe, you could detail other ways to get abroad such as ferries and airlines.

For writing that relies on a range of sources, you will find that it can help if you occasionally move away from generalisations and bring in some personal anecdotes or actual experiences as they are more likely to make readers feel involved.

You only need to talk to a few people or carry out a few small tasks for this to work, for example:

- an article about travel preparations – describe having a go at packing your own case whilst keeping to an airline's tight weight limit
- a general look at woodcraft courses – get someone to show you how to us a hammer and chisel and recount your experiences, or interview a woodwork tutor
- a book on care in the community – work as a volunteer and visit and talk to a few elderly people or social workers for first-hand quotations

EXERCISE 2
1. *Do you already have an idea for a non-fiction project?*
2. *If so, which of the above categories does it fall into?*
3. *Is there one way you could improve the material you have in mind e.g. by adding in some interviews, reference material or personal anecdotes?*

HOW TO MAKE MONEY FROM NON-FICTION

There are many different ways to make money from non-fiction writing. Here are ten examples:

1. Win the star prize for a letter or the award of "letter of the month", which can take the form of cheques, goods or services worth anything from £25 to over £80. Depending on the publication, prizes can be relevant gadgets, baby goods or craft materials, books, flowers, stationery, drink or vouchers for days out.

2. Have a number of letters, recipes, tips, 'photographs that tell a story' or general short pieces published that can pay £5 - £25

3. Receive payment for magazine or newspaper articles of around £50 - £150 each, depending on their length and the financial state of the publication

4. Win prizes in writing competitions. As an example, at the time of writing the Daily Telegraph pays £200 a week for the best "Just Back" 500-word travel article

5. Publish and sell books. You will either receive royalties (usually around 10% of the cover price) from mainstream publishers or up to the full sale price if you self-publish with or without the help of ebook publishers, and some publishers pay an advance which you keep even if the book never sells. The ideal is to write a book that is sure to sell – for example, a must-have textbook. You could also earn money by contributing a chapter to someone else's book.

6. Write books that are bought by libraries and benefit from library lending payments (PLR – see later)

7. Write articles or books whose content is copied by others and earn copying fees (ALCS – see later)

8. Be employed by someone to write for them on a regular basis, so that it is your salary rather than word count that is important

9. Produce course materials

10. Write enough features for websites to start receiving a small percentage of advertising revenue, or be paid per contribution.

It should be noted that small publishers of obscure magazines and journals with very low circulation figures as well as local newspapers are often not in a position to pay writers for their contributions. But if you want to build up your credibility and a useful portfolio of published work, it can be a very positive decision to write for free at least at the start of a writing career.

NON-FICTION OUTLETS

When you set out to write non-fiction, the three most common outlets for your work are magazines and newspapers, websites or books. Although this guide concentrates on such areas, there are other opportunities for getting your non-fiction writing into the public domain that you should look out for. For example, you could write:

- Pamphlets and leaflets for a wide range of organisations including tourist boards, charities or museums
- Film company material, radio talks or TV documentary scripts
- Photography links
- Background notes or profiles on CDs, DVDs or theatre programmes
- Commissioned work for PR companies, local shops or other organisations who want publicity or background material to offer their clients and customers
- Pithy sayings or jokes in greetings cards.

When it comes to format, once you have identified your target readership it is possible to offer the same material in print or electronically – either online or in the form of downloadable content. On the Web, you may need to design headlines and captions to attract traffic to the site and to organise the content so that it is enticing enough for people who are just browsing to make them stay and read the page (see Chapter 9 for further information). But once you have done that, similar content is often just as appropriate whichever medium you choose.

PITCHING YOUR WORK

In most cases, if you want a publisher to bring out your work, you need to persuade them that yours is worth publishing. This is known as pitching, and it is a very important process. However beautifully you write, if you can't find an editor who wants to publish your writing there are few ways for you to reach an audience by yourself. It may be simple to set up a website or start a blog; to use your PC and print leaflets to leave in shops; or to bring out a book fairly cheaply (see later), but as an unknown writer it is very difficult to make money this way. That is because it can be hard to get taken seriously or even to be noticed by the general public if you go it alone. There is so much writing out there that it is often only by contributing to well-known publications or through the support of the marketing departments and sales reps of mainstream publishers that your work will be read.

WHAT TO SEND

Aside from letters or short fillers, you don't usually send a finished manuscript to an editor except with humorous articles where it is hard to summarise their content. Instead, you send them your description of what you want to write together with a justification for sending it to them and your credentials as the author. Once they agree to go ahead, you can establish all the details including word count, deadlines, illustrations etc. before writing or completing your manuscript. .

There are certain technical terms you need to become familiar with when seeking a publisher and these include:

- Content editor – someone who manages and edits web page content
- Commissioning editor – the person who identifies books or other material to publish
- Submission or query letter– your selling document where you pitch the idea for a book, article or other content to an editor

- Proposal – the book or article details such as an overview, a detailed outline of the chapters, a sample of your writing and some form of biography or CV

EXAMPLE
Here is what Interweave Press ask for in a book proposal:
A one page overview of your book idea explaining the basic concept, what makes it special, and how is it different from the competitive books on the market
• define who the audience is for the book, including skill level
• a short bio detailing your qualifications for writing the book
• an outline or table of contents for the book including a list of techniques and projects covered
• a sample project or chapter that will be representative of the book and your writing style

THE PROCESS

Whatever type of material you want published, there are certain steps to go through. Follow these to give yourself the best chance of having work accepted.

Step 1: Follow the guidelines

Having identified the most appropriate publication or website for your material, locate and read their submission guidelines and then provide all the details they ask for. This is crucial as disobeying their instructions can lead to automatic rejection even if your work would be perfect for them. Sometimes there is a link on the company's website where you can read or download the guidelines, or you can phone and ask for them to be sent to you.

If they don't produce any, find the publisher of a comparable publication and read theirs as they will probably ask for similar information and this will help you identify what sort of material to send.

Whether sending by email or post, make sure you have presented your manuscripts in the correct format e.g. double spaced, if requested, appropriate details on the cover sheet or in headers and footers, how the pages are clipped together etc, so that you give editors no reason to reject your offering.

Nowadays, most companies will accept query letters and even manuscripts by email, but check that they don't state categorically that they want them in writing only.

Step 2: Locate an editor to pitch to

When approaching magazines, newspapers, journals or book publishers you need to find the name of the commissioning, assistant or overall editor for your type of material. They will either be listed in a staff contacts list or you can phone the company and try to find the name.

If you are writing for a series or section where material is regularly elicited from freelance writers or the publication's readers, it is usually clear where to send your contribution. If not, it is very important to contact a named person if you can; otherwise your letter or email may disappear into the bowels of the company. Sometimes there is a general email or postal address set up for writers to send their ideas to in the first place which should be manned by appropriate staff. If you can find out nothing and want to write to them with your ideas, address any letter to the commissioning editor and name an imaginary department or suitable category e.g. "children's reference" or "art and craft" to help target your submission to the right person.

Websites may also name their content editor, or there may be a general email for submitting ideas. Very often, websites are seeking writers to fill their pages and so there could be an online process for submitting work. For example, the website Howopia publishes 'how to' guides and there is a link labelled "Write for us" that will take you to a page setting out the whole process in some detail.

Step 3: Check back at the appropriate time

Editors receive huge numbers of submissions and it is hard to know how long to leave things before you check that: a) they have received your proposal, if you never had an acknowledgement, and b) if they know when a final decision will be made. Normally if the original editor likes your idea and it is for a long piece, a series or an entire book, the idea will be presented at one or more publishers' meetings and the process can be quite long-winded.

I wouldn't recommend contacting them until three or four weeks have passed to ask about the final decision, but then it is reasonable to do so. This is especially true if you want to send the same idea to a different publisher as it could be important that you get timely feedback on whether they are considering your work seriously or not. A quick phone call to ask this question is perfectly acceptable and would never stop an editor from publishing. Don't go for the hard sell at this stage if they don't say yes straight away, though, or it might push them into a rejection just to get rid of you.

Step 4: Respond appropriately

If you are lucky enough to have your idea accepted, your aim should be to produce work in the correct format and of the right length before the deadline that has been set. If writing a book, there is no need to wait for the contract to arrive before you start drafting, once you are clear about the project, but when the paperwork does arrive, read it carefully before signing (see Chapter 8 for further details about contracts).

Always check back with your editor if you have any concerns about your rights or what is entailed. As far as word count goes, from my experience the length of articles is very important as there is only limited space on a magazine page, but book length can be more flexible. Don't panic if your word count doesn't match exactly – it is often only a guess anyway. Just tell them the situation and discuss how, if necessary, you can cut or add to meet their minimum or maximum requirements.

You will normally end up working with one or two editors with whom you may build up a long and harmonious relationship. Bearing in mind that they might well commission further work from you in the future, it is very important to treat them with great respect.

Never delay responding if they ask for information or drafts. Even if you are not ready, always contact them and explain. There is nothing worse than a deafening silence, when no-one knows if their communications have been received, or letting them down by not delivering without having given clear warning as to possible delays.

Try to take on board their comments and suggestions, unless you feel very strongly that you can justify not doing so. Although your writing is a personal thing, if you want your work published the suggestions made by experienced editors for cutting, changing or adding material are likely to be sensible and commercially sound.

MULTIPLE PITCHING

Everyone in publishing will tell you it is bad form to send out more than one submission at a time. That's because they don't want to spend time discussing your work and agreeing to go ahead only to hear that you have turned them down in favour of a better offer from a competing publication.

If editors worked fast and gave you a response in a timely manner, I think that would be justified. But when you can wait months to hear if your article or book proposal has been accepted, it isn't fair on writers. For that reason, I cannot see anything wrong in sending out two or three query letters or book submissions at the same time, knowing how hard it is to find just one editor willing to publish. As long as your submissions are reasonably concise, it shouldn't take them very long to consider your idea at least as to whether it would be viable for them or not, and the worst that can happen is that an editor who is keen will lose one potential article or book if they respond too slowly and you end up working with a rival. Considering how many writing ideas don't come to fruition, as long as you turn down the rejected editor in a pleasant and constructive way it shouldn't be a problem.

Clearly if you have worked with an editor in the past and submit a new proposal that fits in with their publishing requirements, it is sensible to wait for them to decide if it is appropriate (and check with them directly) before going to a rival. Otherwise, you could sour a good relationship for the sake of a few weeks.

Just a note on submitting readers' letters to newspapers and magazines: you wouldn't expect acknowledgement of these as so many are received every week. However, you may have to wait a month or two before you know that your own contribution has been printed, and that depends on whether you are able to get hold of a copy of the actual letters page. Perhaps the best advice, if you don't see the publication regularly, is to change your letter enough for it to be a different one before sending it to anyone else. Then it won't matter if both versions end up in print.

EXERCISE 3
1. *Think of any topic you could write a book about. If you have absolutely no ideas at the moment, think of a topic closely related to one of your hobbies, qualifications or a job you have had.*
2. *Use any search engine or visit the library and find the details of one publisher of a book on the same subject.*
3. *Use any means to find the name and contact details for the appropriate commissioning editor.*

CH 2.

FINDING YOUR SUBJECT

It is often a good idea when starting out on a writing career, or if you want this to be just an enjoyable hobby, to write about what you know – unless you are strongly motivated towards a particular topic. The confidence that personal knowledge or experience can give you means you can be more relaxed about your writing and can concentrate on the style and presentation without worrying quite so much about the subject matter or having to spend a large amount of time on research.

(To prove that this is what happens, imagine that you have been asked to write a book that must be on one of two subjects – either a country you have lived in all or most of your life, or a country you have never visited or know anything about. Both are huge projects, but with a country you know well, at least you can start to think about the topics to cover and what you might want to say. The learning curve when covering a completely unknown place is going to be far, far steeper.)

If you try to list all your specialist knowledge off the top of your head, you are likely to hit a brick wall quite quickly, and so you need some self-analysis techniques that will encourage lateral thinking and help jog your memory.

ROLES

One way is to think back over all the roles you have ever held in your life. These are going to fall into a number of different categories:

- Relationships – as a son/daughter, father/mother, aunt/uncle, grandparent, child, brother/sister, husband/wife/partner

- Unpaid in the family – driver (for the school run, spouse to work, yourself out shopping, family or friend to the airport etc), cook (family meals, for school or church fundraising, to help out a relative who was ill), teacher (help with homework, teach someone to drive, read, use a computer etc), dresser (child, elderly relative), hairdresser (child or relative's hair), financier (household budget, plan family holidays), DIY expert
- Work – secretary, nurse, sales assistant, carpenter, CEO, self-employed book-keeper, engineer, translator etc.
- Leisure – club secretary or chairman, newsletter writer, tutor, life guard, rabbit breeder, painter, TV critic, learner (on courses)
- Others – e.g. campaigner, political party member, environmental protester, volunteer, pensioner, tourist, photographer, burglar, busker etc.

EXERCISE 4

1. *Spend 5 – 10 minutes writing down all the roles you remember holding.*
2. *Take two or three of these and write a story you remember from when you were IN each of these roles. For example: as a daughter or son - visiting care homes with your elderly parent; as a snake breeder – trying to incubate your first eggs; as a twenty something learning how to ski; as a member of the PTA – raising money for the school by organising an art exhibition; or as a new recruit, learning about life on a cruise ship.*
3. *If possible, classify the stories according to the type of experience you had or how you think the subject could be treated for non-fiction writing e.g. Care homes – opinion piece about what they are like; factual piece about what to look for or how to pay the fees; local interest featuring care homes in your area; a review – comparing three different care homes; or part of a wider look at where elderly people can live. Learning to ski: "how to" article; personal story; travel piece etc.*

4. *Keep these notes and use them for later exercises.*
5. *If this is a productive exercise for you, continue adding more stories to your bank of examples that you can call on later.*

CURRICULUM VITAE

Most people at some stage will have applied for jobs and so you are likely to have needed to produce a CV. This is a goldmine for a writer as it will contain details of your past education, training and work experience that it is easy to forget as you grow older. If you had managed to produce a list of 10 work roles, for example, in the exercise above, looking at your CV may help you add another 2 – 20 to that list. Certainly many temporary, short-term or holiday jobs might be revealed that you had completely forgotten about, and they can be very helpful in identifying experiences you could write about. In the same way, favourite school subjects, clubs and societies, college or university involvement, one-day training courses or time as a home-schooled child can all be added to your portfolio of life experiences.

When the time is ripe, you may be able to use these stories or the knowledge and experience you gained as the basis for a non-fiction piece.

EXAMPLE
In 1989 - 1990 I was on a teacher training course and, during that time, had an interesting experience trying to tell a class of seven-year olds a story rather than read to them from a picture book.

In 2006, the Times Educational Supplement printed a letter I sent them about the incident as the paper was featuring articles about storytelling in schools at that time. Although it had happened 16 years before, my story was relevant enough to seem a modern tale and there was no mention of the actual date in my letter.

EXERCISE 5
1. *If you have an old CV, dig it out and update it. If not, draw up a draft CV and try to list not only the places you studied or*

worked but also your actual tasks, successes and responsibilities.

2. *Look through your CV and find as many examples of organisations, job types, subject knowledge or roles as you can that look promising as something to write about.*

3. *Identify one amusing, sad or exciting incident you can remember and write it down in as much detail as possible.*

4. *Keep this as a potential story for a magazine or newspaper letter or article.*

THE TIME LINE

A time line is simply an annotated representation of your entire life where you write in all the significant events, activities, people and places you can remember. Although this exercise is usually carried out when planning an autobiography, it is also valuable in helping you remember forgotten aspects of your life for other purposes.

Whatever age you are now, if you divide your life roughly by 6 you will have a manageable number of time periods to work with. For example, if you are now 35, you would have the following 6 periods:

0 – 6
7 – 12
13 – 18
19 - 24
25 – 30
31 – Now

You can also add the actual years as you often remember events by the date rather than your own age. So you would have the years 0 – 6 and the dates 1977 – 1983.

A quick way to create the time line is not actually to draw a line but to use six different pieces of paper. At the top of each one, write your start and end ages and the dates in years. Now you can start brainstorming and writing down all the significant things you can remember taking place during those different time periods.

For example, you could write down:

- family births, marriages and deaths
- different schools attended or other periods of education
- where you were living
- pets
- awards and prizes
- holidays
- illnesses
- significant moments that spring to mind
- associated pieces of music
- successes and failures
- political events affecting your life, and
- anything else that comes to mind.

To start with, you may feel this has little to do with non-fiction writing, but as you continue to work on your time line and build up a large bank of memories, you will start to see patterns emerging, specialist knowledge being revealed and interests and skills being identified.

As an example of how useful the exercise can be, imagine finding that you have written down some of these experiences:

- buying a boat
- becoming an engineering apprentice
- flying your first plane
- going bankrupt
- setting up a telescope
- marrying your childhood sweetheart
- being evacuated
- teaching English in Africa
- learning how to walk with a prosthetic leg
- finding out you were adopted

Don't they all sound like articles you might read in a magazine, or even subjects that could be expanded into a book?

Once again, having identified a topic, if you think about it you can probably come up with several different ways it might be treated, from opinion pieces to factual information or humorous writing.

EXERCISE 6
1. *Create your own time line.*
2. *Complete as much as you can, and continue over the next few weeks.*
3. *Pick out any topics that could form the basis for an article or book.*
4. *Select one example of an event – e.g. a wedding or birth - that you know something about (perhaps you were the bride, bridegroom, best man, vicar, wedding photographer, guest, midwife, in-law, new parent or sibling) and draft out a narrative that might be appropriate for a Wedding or Babies magazine or the local paper. If possible, try to include an amusing incident that you heard about or can recall happening.*

Here are two actual examples of the first paragraphs of articles from:

The Daily Express: "Most couples expect to receive the obligatory toaster among their wedding presents, along with the towels, sheets and cutlery. But newlyweds Clair and Stuart sat dumbfounded as they unwrapped no less than 24."

Best magazine: "Janice, 62 loves the thrill of finding a new hubby, so much so she's on the hunt for number SEVEN. The mum-of-two admits she was so obsessed with being a wife she simply married anyone who asked. But her obsession with finding a husband meant she kept marrying the wrong guy again, and again, and again..."

CH. 3

BRINGING YOUR WRITING TO LIFE

In fiction writing, it is well known that there are techniques for lifting dull prose and bringing life to a boring story. But these techniques are equally effective and have a vital role to play in non-fiction. This is especially true for any descriptive or opinion pieces or those involving a number of characters.

One "in-between" area of non-fiction is referred to as creative non-fiction and is defined as writing that "uses literary styles and techniques". It is employed particularly in travel, biography, opinion, food and persuasive writing. Such 'fiction-style' non-fiction only differs from fiction in that it is based on fact rather than the imagination.

WRITING STORIES

Surprisingly enough, stories are a major part of non-fiction. This is not because you need to have a plot but because you have to find a way to engage readers. Pure facts, description or statistics are not going to do that half as well as involving them in the narrator's or other people's stories.

This means that, once you have decided on your topic and the major features you want to include, it is worth seeing if you can add in a story, rather than keep the whole piece neutral and potentially leave your readers uninvolved and unmoved.

The key is often to find one or two people and concentrate on them. It could be you, or someone in the crowd or in your group, an official or just someone you meet.

EXAMPLE

Several people were recently asked to describe a football match for a writing exercise. Most pieces were well written but kept everything general – all content related to "the crowd" or "the team". A less polished article was the most effective because it focused on the goalkeeper, describing how he became despondent after allowing an early goal but then recovered to save a late penalty. Following his story retained the tension and interest in the piece.

Here are some examples of how this could work if you were writing about a Jubilee street party for the local paper:

- Feature an elderly resident who can remember other street parties and ask her to compare them
- Watch a family group and describe how the adults and children behave, what they eat etc.
- Concentrate on behind the scenes: tell readers about the people bringing out tea urns, clearing up afterwards or those hanging out the bunting
- Compare the experience of one elderly and one young couple
- Describe the enjoyment of one particular child
- Put yourself in the piece and remember your first street party
- Describe how someone's dog behaves
- Follow the music – describe records chosen, live bands, dancing, children's choirs etc.

EXERCISE 7

1. *Go somewhere busy like a market, festival, fair or sports match.*
2. *Take as many notes as you can so that you can write a piece about the event.*
3. *See if you can find someone or something to focus on that you can use to tell a story.*

4. *Write up your piece. If you want to experiment, write two pieces – one straightforward but neutral and the other including your story so that you can compare the two.*

BEING CLEAR

Everything you write will be crystal clear to you personally, but unless you are very careful, and especially if you introduce a large cast or have a lot of ground to cover and choose to move backwards and forwards in time, your readers may not be fully in the picture and may become confused. (If you have ever read a book where you suddenly find yourself wondering who is talking, or when an event took place, you will know what I mean!)

The only way to prevent confusion arising is to check that, at least implicitly, you have included as much as you can of the following information:

Who is this part about? When you first mention someone by name or introduce a new character, think about whether their role or relationships are clear. If not, try to think of a way to introduce them to readers so that they are aware of the person's significance to the story or why they have been introduced.

What is going on? A common mistake made by new writers is to overwhelm their readers with too much detail because they cannot bear to leave anything out. If you realise this and try to cut back some of the material, there is a danger that you'll go too far the other way. (This is often the case when a film is made from a book and the audience literally lose the plot.) Ideally, make sure that readers are given enough information to understand exactly what is happening but don't give them more than is necessary.

Why is something included, or why was a particular decision made? A straightforward descriptive piece may not need reasons, but it can be important for readers to understand exactly why something happened.

For example, there may be a particular point you want to make or a lesson to be learned. If this is the case, you don't want it obscured.

Where did an event take place? Each time you write a new scene, check that your readers will know where everything is taking place if it is an important aspect of the story. Also remember that the setting for any scene can also be very important, so include small details that will show this clearly.

When did an event take place? It is easy to forget that if your work covers a lengthy period of time, your readers could end up confused as to where they are in the story. In particular, it can be very irritating if it isn't clear that an important event took place before or after a significant event or if someone or something that is featured was young or old. Obviously you won't want to mention ages and dates every paragraph or chapter, but if your readers need to know when an event took place, make sure you include these facts somewhere.

How did it come about? If your writing is good, your readers will hopefully be intrigued and this means they will be asking themselves "How" questions – How did it get broken? How did he get out of the camp? How did she look when she met her family again? Even if you only want to answer these questions bit by bit or later in the story, make sure they ARE answered and your readers are not left frustrated and unsatisfied.

COME TO YOUR SENSES

Most writers are good at describing what they see, but few go further than that. Yet humans have five senses: sight, sound, touch, taste and smell, and employing more than one sense in your writing will usually improve it as the contents will become more vivid to readers.

Obviously the senses you select have to be appropriate and you need to be subtle when introducing more than one or two, but if you can, try to expand your writing now and again to incorporate different senses and you will certainly lift a boring piece.

EXERCISE 8

1. *If you find the idea of writing about touch or taste difficult, have a go at this exercise commonly known as the "lemon sherbet game".*

2. *Find some sweets (or chocolate, cheese or fruit) that is in some type of packaging. Place this in front of you.*

3. *Firstly, write down exactly what you see.*

4. *Unwrap the food and write down exactly what you can hear as you do so and as you handle the contents.*

5. *Smell the food and packaging and write down what it smells like.*

6. *Feel it carefully with your fingers and then write down the sensations you experience and the texture and firmness of the food.*

7. *Finally, taste the food slowly and write down what it tastes like.*

SMALL DETAILS

Perhaps the most important piece of advice I can give you as a writer is this: it is the small details that will bring your work to life.

Boring and bland passages, if you come across any in the books or articles you read, usually have little or no variety or 'hook' to catch your interest, and they tend to be full of generalisations. They leave you feeling uninvolved and uninterested and may make you close the publication altogether.

Without including long detailed descriptions, being specific and mentioning immediately recognisable objects will often add a sparkle to your writing, as well as help readers visualise the scene and bring it to life. Quirky little facts are a particularly valuable device.

EXERCISE 9

1. *Find a long article in a magazine or newspaper that you think is well written and maintains your interest.*

2. *Look for any small factual details. See how the writer uses descriptions of items such as clothes, household objects, mechanical workings or architectural features to help you visualise the place or objects as you read.*

When dealing with dry facts and figures, for example, it can be more interesting for readers if you can find images that help put them in context:

To get across the size of a blue whale, one writer told readers that its tongue weighs as much as an elephant, (rather than it weighs about 125 tons)

To explain how much lead is in a pencil, another writer said that it can draw a line around 20 miles in length (rather than just that the lead in a pencil is normally about 17cm long with a diameter of 0.2cm).

Instead of describing someone driving a car, you can use the make and even model to help build character and enable readers to picture the scene:
A large, silver Chevy, or
A small, cherry-red mini, or
An old-fashioned London taxi

Most readers would instantly be able to see the vehicle in their minds. So such details can only add to your story – particularly if there is a contrast between a character and the car they choose to drive. Details can also save a great deal of text, for example by instantly placing your characters in America or London.

EXERCISE 10
1. Take any half or one-page piece of writing you have completed that you feel is quite good and that is open to this type of technique.
2. Go through and see if there are any extra details you could add to make the scene even more vivid.

POINT OF VIEW

You will know that there are a number of different viewpoints a piece can be written from:

First person: *"I noticed that everyone was wearing ...... "*

Second person: *"You will notice that everyone is wearing...."*

Third person limited (staying with one character for each section or chapter): *"He was trying hard not to cry ...."*

If you aren't sure which is best, write a couple of paragraphs from each point of view before making your final decision. Clearly first person is the most intimate but it can not only restrict what you cover but may also tempt you to put too much of yourself into the writing. Third person limited is probably the favourite for general articles.

An unusual point of view is third person objective. Here, the observer is neutral and uninvolved and so this should only be a deliberate choice if you want to keep your distance as the narrator e.g. *"Children were running around getting excited about the equipment."*

SHOW NOT TELL

When you tell readers how the characters in your tales are feeling or behaving, or what condition objects are in, your audience has only a passive role in your writing and it can lead to a lack of involvement or even boredom. If you make your readers work at the piece so that they have to recreate the feelings, behaviour or conditions for themselves, you are far more likely to maintain their interest. This allows your audience to have the satisfaction of reaching its own conclusions.

You do this by showing the feelings or behaviour in your writing. This comes from your description of body language, speech and actions or the detailed condition of things. If you are not sure what I mean, just ask yourself the question: "how do you know he/she/it felt.... Or she/he/it was.......?" when you have used descriptive adjectives or adverbs. If you put your answer into words, you will be showing not telling.

For example:

Telling: "The tourist guide was tired and bored with us all."
How do you know he was tired and bored?
Showing: "The guide yawned widely, not even bothering to cover his mouth with a hand, lay back in his seat and closed his eyes."

Telling: "The priest banged the gong loudly."
How do you know it was loud?
Showing: "As the priest banged the gong, several members of the coach party put their hands over their ears and the reverberations I felt in my head continued for several minutes after he had stopped".

Telling: The jetty was rotten and far too dangerous to walk on.
How do you know it was rotten and dangerous?
Showing: The jetty was in a terrible state. Some of the planks had great chunks missing or were eaten away and the rail was rusty and bent. But there was no other way to reach the boat.

The types of descriptive adjectives you can replace include:
Sizes e.g. large, tall
Shapes e.g. round, angular
Qualities e.g. wicked, kind, funny
Personality e.g. jolly, morose
Ages e.g. young, second-hand
Sound-related e.g. penetrating, quiet
Touch-related e.g. soft, rough
Taste-related e.g. sour, salty

Adverbs are often recognisable as adjectives with the addition of 'ly' e.g. brightly, quietly, beautifully.

> *EXERCISE 11*
> *Write something that shows the meaning of the following:*
> > a. *I felt frightened b. The day was hot c . "Get out of my way" he said angrily. d. When the team appeared, the crowd were ecstatic.*

DIALOGUE

"Do you think dialogue works in non-fiction?" I asked my friend.
"Well, it's a good way to start an article, I suppose."

There is nothing that can provide immediacy more than people's conversations, or recalling what they said and how they said it. Speech, especially set in the context of actual dialogue, can tell readers so much about the people you are describing in terms of their:

Emotions and feelings

Behaviour

Personality

Motives

Hidden agendas

Class

Attitudes

Education

Local roots

It is also one of the best ways to "show not tell" and to move your story on.

As well as the actual words, it is also important to include the tone of voice, body language, dialect, facial expressions and behaviour of the speakers.

Unless you are interviewing someone, or you carry a tape recorder around with you or jot down everything you hear in shorthand, you are unlikely to be able to recall conversations word for word. But as long as you represent speech faithfully in the way you remember it or it is most likely to have been used, it will still convey a true picture of people's personalities and behaviour.

EXAMPLE

To bring colour and vitality to a report on a visit you make to an indoor market, you could include:

- *stallholders' patter*

- *arguments or banter between stallholders and customers*
- *a mother and daughter discussing a purchase*
- *comments overheard on the bus home*
- *a security guard talking to customers*

Having suggested you include dialogue in your work, it is worth noting that you can also have too much. Unless you want to turn your material into a play, you do need to use it sparingly. Aim for variety and contrast in any written piece by combining the main styles of writing – narrative, action and dialogue – to keep readers engaged and wanting to continue.

EXAMPLE

Here is a short extract from a winning travel piece written by Pam Tibbetts in the Daily Telegraph about visiting Australia:

I'm alive. Tubes everywhere. Stapled together from navel to groin, but who cares. I'm overwhelmed by the competence, compassion and care of the hospital staff. My nurse has the loveliest smile. I ask where she's from. Marysville. A faint whiff of smoke in the air reminds me that bush fires are still raging to the north. Casualties still rising. I feel guilty taking up bed space.

"Isn't that one of the towns destroyed last week?" I ask.

"Yes. I got married there six months ago. The church has gone."

"What about your family?"

"They don't live there now, but friends do. They're missing. I've been trying to locate them, but…"

Her words hang in the air like the distant smoke. "I'm so sorry," I say. She smiles her warm smile. "Just think about getting better. You're lucky to be alive."

EXERCISE 12

1. *Go somewhere like a café or park where you can sit and overhear conversations without being obvious.*
2. *Write down as much as you can of what is said and how people are saying it.*

3. *At home, try to pick one or more quotations or a piece of dialogue that sums up the people and that might enhance a piece of writing and then use it in a short descriptive piece about the place you were sitting.*

CONVENTIONS FOR DIALOGUE

When including dialogue in a piece of work, the normal conventions are as follows:

- Surround all spoken words with "quote marks" and only add final quote marks when the same person finishes speaking, even if their speech extends over more than one paragraph.

- Place a comma at the end of a piece of dialogue, before the end quote marks and details of who is speaking e.g. "You were quite right," she said, putting on her coat.

- Place a comma in this way and also before the start of new quote marks if your speaker's details are positioned between two passages. For example: "I was always told," John smiled at Jessie as he spoke, "that little girls should be seen and not heard."

- Start a new paragraph every time a different person speaks

- Make absolutely clear who is talking. Sometimes you won't need any more than the words themselves, but if several people are joining in a discussion you don't want your reader confused about who said what to whom. One simple way is occasionally to include someone's name so that readers will know who is being spoken to. For example:
  "Sheila, darling, I really think that is a silly idea."

- Now and again, change the position for details of who is speaking. As well as in the middle between parts of sentences, you can place these details at either the beginning or end of a spoken passage e.g. Jim spoke quietly: "Don't force me to do this." "Don't be daft, it will be fine," answered Harry.

Although you may want to try a range of different words, using *said* is perfectly acceptable on a regular basis. Otherwise you can fall into the trap of looking as if you are trying too hard. The constant and relentless use of cried, shouted, whispered, screamed etc can become irritating.

Take care not to use dialogue as a simple replacement for description. Try to use it for a purpose.

EXERCISE 13
1. *To practise writing dialogue, take any short piece of dialogue you have overheard or that you hear on the radio or TV.*
2. *Develop it into an imaginary conversation.*
3. *Try to separate sections of actual speech with actions, descriptions and scene setting so that an entire picture of the scene is presented to readers.*

SIMILES AND METAPHORS

There are two figures of speech that fiction writers are always encouraged to include in their work and which are equally valid for good quality non-fiction writing. These are similes and metaphors.

The reason for using them is that they create an image in the mind of the reader far more effectively than plain description and very often will save you having to describe something in any detail at all. In particular, they can encourage people to visualize objects or understand concepts that may be abstract and difficult to describe, by evoking a more familiar picture or experience.

The key to including them successfully in your writing is to try and avoid using too many of the terribly clichéd examples (over-worn phrases that we all instantly recognise) and to use them sparingly, with care. The best writers introduce them in fresh and imaginative ways but even if you cannot create your own, the odd well-placed example can still lift a piece of writing and make it livelier and more memorable.

If you want to read hundreds of examples, both similes and metaphors have been collected together into a book called "Eyes like Butterflies" by Terence Hodgson.

SIMILES

These involve comparing two dissimilar things that have one key aspect in common. (The more outrageous the difference between the objects, the more exciting these can be.) The joining words are usually as......as, than or like.

For example:
The meringue was as light as a cloud
His socks smelled like ripe cheese
She was as prickly as a little cat
My fingers were so cold they felt like icicles
He was happier than King Canute when the tide turned.

> *EXERCISE 14*
> 1. *Create similes for the following ideas:*
>   a.   *The weather was* ....
>   b.   *He coughed* ....
>   c.   *The atmosphere in the restaurant was* ....
> 2. *Look back at any descriptive piece you have written and try to rewrite a part to include a simile.*

METAPHORS

These involve understanding one thing in terms of another (as if it actually IS something else) rather than using the words as or like. They are harder to employ but can be even more exciting in a piece of writing. Often, once introduced you can sustain a metaphor through several passages to build up the image for readers.

Examples of metaphors:
The plate was filled with clouds of meringue
He was burning with anger
That year, a whole new crop of trainees joined my department

Creating your own metaphor

There are four simple steps you can take if you want to create your own metaphors:
1. Decide on the subject or idea you want to write about
2. Identify the emotion, image or atmosphere you want to evoke such as beauty, speed, colour, how frightening it was or how much joy it brought.
3. Think of a separate object or idea that is normally associated with being beautiful, frightening, fast etc.
4. Put the two together

EXAMPLES

a. A lovely morning in summer will have a blue sky. Cornflowers are blue so your metaphor is: "It was a cornflower blue morning"

b. For a train journey you may want to convey its speed. Bullets and arrows both go fast and so you could combine the two images and write about a train journey where: "....the train was released from the station and shot towards its target."

EXERCISE 15

1. *Choose 3 from the following list of ideas or objects and create a metaphor for each one:*
   a. *A funeral*
   b. *Sitting an exam*
   c. *Giving a speech*
   d. *A pet*

e. *A long awaited phone call*
f. *My computer*
g. *My favourite room*

MIXED METAPHORS

These happen when two different and often conflicting images are evoked to describe the same concept. They are to be avoided as they are usually quite ridiculous. For example: He shot the wind out of her saddle (rather than sails).

****

CH. 4

WRITING FOR MAGAZINES, JOURNALS AND NEWSPAPERS

With so many daily, fortnightly, weekly and monthly publications constantly being printed (as well as web pages being updated) both here and across the English-speaking world, there is great scope for freelancers. Editors all need copy, whether it is timeless articles or features based on current happenings.

To help you research possible markets and discover new publishers, several writing publications including Freelance Market News and Writing Magazine provide up-to-date advice. They cover new outlets, changes of policy within existing publishers, what types of contribution are being sought and who may no longer be welcoming advances from freelancers. The publications also provide details of named editors together with their email addresses and telephone numbers. At the start of a writing career, it is well worth subscribing to one of these for a few months.

WHAT YOU COULD WRITE

There are probably about nine or ten main types of contribution received from an unknown writer that an editor might consider publishing.

> *EXERCISE 16*
> 1. *Find one or two different types of magazine*
> 2. *Identify all the non-fiction content that you could possibly write*
> 3. *Group the contributions into general categories*

When you carry out this exercise across a broad range of magazines you will find that most of them contain similar slots you could fill, including:

- Letters
- Articles
- Fillers e.g. recipes, tips, snippets of information
- Regular columns e.g. Questions & Answers (Q & A), diary entries, opinion pieces, facts about.... , forthcoming events
- Personal stories
- Reviews – festivals, books, entertainment, restaurants, food & drink, appliances or more specialist items e.g. boats, bikes, cars etc.
- Interviews or profiles
- Travel guides
- Celebrity gossip
- Historical or local interest pieces
- Photo-stories with captions or short accompanying entries

Although journals and newspapers are produced for different purposes, they too fill space with many of the same types of copy and so the potential for freelancers is enormous. Each publication will obviously have a slightly different requirement so look at as many examples as you can to find out exactly what is sought.

EXAMPLE
On their website at www.ctc.org.uk , Cycling Magazine has the following list of contributions they accept, although some only from members of the organisation:
Letters
Questions to be answered
Travellers' Tales
Obituaries

Product reviews
Articles
Photographs

INTERNATIONAL MARKETS

To broaden your scope and add possible markets, don't forget the overseas press. Use the Internet to locate magazine and journal publishers and contact them as you would publishers within the UK. If possible, get hold of some of their publications first as there may be important differences you need to be aware of. A few examples of overseas publications in English include:

- The Australian Women's Weekly (monthly) and Woman's Day (weekly)
- America's Life magazine
- Middle East Glass Magazine
- Car India
- NAG - South African computing magazine
- Wilderness – New Zealand outdoors magazine

Obviously, cultural and social differences and values need to be taken into account when writing for an overseas audience, as well as your use of the English language. This is particularly true when it comes to jargon, technical terms or shorthand. Some words may either be misunderstood or, worse, misinterpreted. For example, the word "billions" has a quite different meaning in America or the Far East. You need to check any work aimed at an overseas market particularly carefully.

TYPES OF PUBLICATION

There are a four main ways to classify magazines, journals and newspapers and these are by:

- Target age or type of reader
- Aim – often linked to the identity of the publisher

- Content
- Format

If we analyse the magazine *Yours*, for example, we find:

Target audience - older people, mainly but not exclusively women

Aim – to entertain, inform and sell products

Publishers – multi-media giant Bauer

Content – general

Format – classic glossy magazine cover but uses lower quality paper and images to keep costs down, average 130pp (in 2012 it was £1.40 fortnightly)

Carry out the same exercise on *Classic Bike* and we find:

Target audience – male motorbike enthusiasts

Aim – to entertain, advertise and inform

Publishers – Emap, part of a large publishing and events business

Content – specialist bikes

Format – classic glossy magazine, 114 pp with numerous colour photos (in 2012 it was £2.80 per month)

WHO ARE THE READERS?

Whenever you write something, it is vital to have the reader in mind. This is especially true for magazine or newspaper features as there is usually a huge audience of loyal readers who have been buying the publication for years. No editor wants to alienate them by printing an inappropriate feature and so they are simply not going to accept work if it is obviously aimed at the wrong audience.

You will find numerous clues to the typical reader in just one issue of a magazine, and when you are advised to "read the publication before submitting work" it is precisely for this reason: so that you are able to identify your audience, (as well as to understand the way they like their material presented).

- Does the magazine title tell you anything?
- What is on the cover?

- Is there any form of mission statement from the editor, at the front?
- Does the scope and content of articles, columns or other features target an identifiable readership?
- What is being advertised?
- Who is featured or profiled?
- What prizes are offered for competitions or star letters?
- What are the letters about?
- What type of review is included?
- Do the photographs or product examples give you any further ideas?
- If there is an online presence, is there more information here about their readership or philosophy?

EXERCISE 17

1. *Examine the entire contents of one magazine, journal or paper of your choice.*
2. *Describe the typical reader.*

When I tried this with one magazine, *Saga*, I found:

- The title suggests it is aimed at readers of historical fiction
- A well-known female celebrity of middle age is on the cover
- Articles cover money, music, writing your autobiography, Christmas outfits for women, cookery, drink, gardening, 60s fashion, dieting, diabetes and owning a woodland. There are also several pages of friendship and "dating" advertisements for people over 60
- Adverts include many aspirational and expensive items of furniture and clothing but also medicines, food home delivery, equipment and independent living establishments all aimed at the over 50s

- Profiles include Sheila Hancock (79), Sir David Attenborough (86), Tom Waits (62) and Caryn Franklin (52)
- The major prize is a Baltic cruise for two
- Letter writers often mention their age (usually over 50) and topics cover living without a computer, going on a cruise and reminiscences. Problem pages include advice on children leaving home, family Christmas and staying faithful at 70.
- There are reviews of books, theatre, films and whiskey.

I am sure you can tell from all this that the magazine covers a wide range of topics but anything you write about, and the advice it might contain, needs to be aimed squarely at readers who are reasonably affluent, of either sex, well educated and over 50.

AIMS AND OBJECTIVES

Most magazines and newspapers are there to provide accurate information, but many use them as a pubic relations vehicle or to try and persuade readers to think in a certain way. Most are funded by advertisements and so they nearly all want to encourage you to buy goods and services. They can be a powerful communication tool – from the organisation to its readers or to encourage communication between readers themselves - and they usually strive to be entertaining at the same time.

Some of the most prestigious publications employ a large staff of writers and this makes it hard for newcomers to get their writing accepted. But there are still hundreds of smaller magazines, papers and journals that depend on contributions from freelancers and even the big glossies and national newspapers encourage contributions such as letters or, from time to time, photos, specific articles or personal stories.

It must also be remembered that nowadays most newspapers and many magazines have a Web presence or digital-only version and these pages also have to be filled.

There are a range of different types of publication you might write for if you were to classify them according to their major aims and objectives, including:

Advertising products, services or the organisation itself to the public

Examples include:

Supermarket magazines such as *Morrisons Magazine*

Those full of classified ads for local trades people e.g. *Round and About*

Airline in-flight magazines such as BA's *High Life*

Providing news

This can be both short term information and in-depth examination and the major examples are local, regional and national newspapers but also some magazines.

Newspapers are important providers not only of news but also of lifestyle and entertainment articles, either in associated magazines or with general articles featured on their inside pages or in special supplements. Some newspapers such as The Guardian and Daily Telegraph have featured specialist "days" when articles and advertisements concentrated on particular subject areas such as education, media, IT or technology, but with the widespread availability of archived articles and job vacancies online, these are probably less relevant today.

Charity or public service publications

These include Advantage, Scotland AgeUK's magazine and Which? published by the campaigning consumer rights organisation.

In-house publications

These keep staff and customers informed about their own organisation e.g. Planet BP or Ariel (the BBC in-house magazine)

Business and trade publications

Nowadays, these are more likely to be referred to as B2B (business to business) publications. They can be full colour print magazines or in simpler journal, newspaper, newsletter or digital formats and are aimed at those in the trade, business or industry. Their aims include keeping readers up-to-date on aspects such as changes in trading law, management appointments, new business opportunities, training and conferences. They are less common in newsagents but should be easy to find out about on the Internet. Examples include Foundry Trade Journal or PR Week.

Association newsletters and magazines

From the Royal Musical Association to Housing Associations, the Arboricultural Association, the University of the 3rd Age (U3A) and the Palaeontological Association, many hundreds of bodies produce newsletters and other publications for their members. These include news, book reviews and opinion pieces where there may be room for a general contribution.

Professional and research journals

Every profession needs to keep those in practice up-to-date and so they usually have their own publication. Nurses, solicitors, teachers, engineers, occupational therapists and social workers are some of the many groups that have their own journals and newspapers and the most well known include Nursing Times and The Times Educational Supplement.

At the same time, there are a number of more specialist publications such as the Journal of Bacteriology or International Journal of Design Engineering in which scientists and engineers publish their research findings. Although these are unlikely to be places for general non-fiction writers, the professional journals and magazines may merit consideration if you have any link to the work involved – either as a professional, a student or as a client of the services.

Science and technology magazines and journals

There are a number of scientific and technical publications aimed more at the general public including National Geographic, The Sky At Night and New Scientist which may also publish features contributed by freelance writers.

Listings magazines

Weekly TV and radio listing magazines, including the Radio Times and What's On TV? inform readers about programming and also the stories behind the programmes. It is possible to have an article published in the more substantial publications and they all welcome and often pay for letters from the general public.

Membership or local area magazines and newsletters

Large and small colleges, churches, societies and clubs set up by enthusiasts such as car clubs, football clubs, gardening clubs and school clubs often produce publications as a way of building a community and they will be happy to receive contributions from interested writers. Some examples include Bournemouth Football Club's The Cherries First Bite magazine, Exon, Exeter College, Oxford University's alumni magazine and M.P.H. - the Journal of the Vincent Owners' Club. There are also local history and regional publications that welcome knowledgeable contributions.

Consumer magazines

The bulk of news-stand publications are consumer magazines, targeting members of the public with a special interest. They aim to entertain, inform and sell products and services and cover everything from current affairs to caravans, cats, cosmetics and computers. Examples include Private Eye, The Week, Good Food, Crafts Beautiful and Computer Weekly.

If you pick a topic you want to write about, there are likely to be several competing magazines covering the same subject matter. To find the titles of less well-known publications to send any contributions to, a good place to start is an online subscription site such as www.magazinesubscriptions.co.uk or www.isubscribe.co.uk

EXERCISE 18

1. *Apart from consumer magazines that are dealt with next, try to get hold of an example from each of the above categories that is of some interest to you.*

2. *If relevant publications in some categories seem hard to identify – consider different aspects of your own life and your possessions and see if there is a publication for members, enthusiasts, owners or other interested parties. For example: do you own a boat, do you volunteer for a charity, do you belong to the Ramblers Association, do you study local history, do you fish, have you ever advertised in a local publication and did you once work for any well-known manufacturers etc?*

3. *Look through each publication and note down the areas where you feel you might be able to contribute a piece.*

SPECIALIST CONTENT

There is probably most scope for new writers if they target one of these specialist consumer magazines or newspapers. Fortunately, almost every interest you can imagine is catered for. Here are some of the many topics they can cover:

Age (Children, Teens, Over 50s)
Animals
Antiques
Architecture
Arts
Babies
Books
Business

Ceramics
Collecting e.g. stamps
Computers
Countryside pursuits
Crafts
Drink
Economics
Education
Fashion
Film
Fitness
Flower arranging
Food
Gardens and gardening
Gossip/celebrities
Hair care
Health
Homes
Humour
Interior Design
Literature
Men
Music
Parenting
Photography
Politics
Religion
Science
Sport
Transport – cars, boats, trains
Weddings
Weight loss
Women
Writing

EXERCISE 19

1. *Look through the above list and add any other categories for which you know there is a magazine, journal or paper.*

2. *Select ALL those you have an interest in or know something about. For example: is it a hobby, your current or a previous job, you studied the subject, you have personal experience or you have some other connection with the subject? (Even after you finish this book, keep adding to your list so that you build up a database of ideas for future contributions.)*

3. *If you have carried out some of the memory jogging exercises in Chapter 2, don't forget to draw on the examples you came up with there.*

4. *Narrow the most significant interests down to THREE with the strongest connection and sketch out an idea for a special interest item you might be able to write about. For example, if you have just had triplets, or taken a baby on holiday, you could write about these for a Baby or Parenting publication. Or if you have recently re-decorated a room, you could write about it for an Interior Design, Craft or Homes magazine.*

FORMAT

Some publications are print only, others just have a Web presence and a growing number of companies publish writing both in print and online or are slowly cutting back on their print versions. It is fairly easy to find mainstay magazines and journals in the newsagents or supermarkets, but you do need to search online for newer outlets as they may provide better opportunities for novice writers.

A few online-only magazine websites available when this book was printed include:

www.boards.co.uk – windsurfing
www.betterbaking.com
www.cateringscotland.com
www.gponline.com – aimed at doctors

Once you locate a suitable publication, carry out exactly the same analysis to identify what type of article or other contribution will work for them and then you can pitch your idea.

GETTING PAID

There are many occasions when contributions are sought and the publication will set out clearly what they will pay, for example when they ask for specific types of photograph, letters or personal stories that fit a certain column.

For other writing, there may be a little room for negotiation but usually an established publisher will let you know the fee they are prepared to pay at the time they accept your work following your initial enquiry. For short pieces, the editor won't normally send out contracts but will say something like: "Our fees are £20 per 1,000 words plus a free copy of the relevant magazine at publication."

In some cases they will request an invoice when the piece appears, but often a cheque will arrive in the post or they will ask for your bank details so that they can pay you direct.

If asked for an invoice, you can keep it extremely simple: put your name and address at the top and then include the publication details, date of the invoice and some type of number such as 001 so that, if you write for them again, you can increase this to 002, 003 etc. In the centre of the page, perhaps in a table, put the title of the piece(s) in one column and the price agreed in another. If you have provided several contributions, list them all and total up the final fee they have agreed to pay.

It is very important, especially if you are quite successful and get a number of articles or other items accepted, that you keep track of your work. Then if you hear nothing some time after publication, you can contact the editor and check on payment.

You must also, of course, keep details of all writing income and expenditure (paper, ink cartridges, manuals etc bought exclusively for your work) for your self-assessment tax form.

SYNDICATION

One good way to make more money from one piece of work is to get it published by different publications. As long as you have agreed the rights to do so this is perfectly acceptable, both in hard copy and online, as long as the print publications or websites are not in direct competition. This is particularly common with newspaper columns but can also apply to one-off articles.

There are three main methods for syndicating work:

- Let your original publisher place the work for you elsewhere
- Sell it directly to other publishers yourself
- Use a syndicate service

Sadly, something you write may well appear in another publication or different form and yet you may get no fee. For example, you should be aware that it is common not to be paid again if a print magazine decides to put your article online after paying for the original; they tend to work on the basis that there is "one flat fee" and they can use your work across all media after that. Subscribing newspapers using a "feed service" can also get hold of copy and reprint it if your original publisher lets it out this way. Or, without reading the small print in your contract or in their terms & conditions, you may find you have given your original publisher exclusive rights so that they can publish or sell your work anywhere else they choose.

If you worry about feed services, ask your publisher not to include your work in feeds. You can still agree to syndication of your individual articles but this time if they are published elsewhere they should agree to pay you a fee.

Self-syndication involves selling your own work to different publishers. An opinion-piece or informative column of general appeal that is published in a local or regional newspaper, for example, could work well in other newspapers without disturbing your relationship with the original editor. (No-one in Glasgow will know if the same column appeared in a Surrey paper, for example. However, do check that the same company doesn't own both papers, or there may be restrictions on its appearance elsewhere.)

When the aim is to gain widespread publication, you must make sure that your contract offers something like "one time non-exclusive rights" to the first publisher so that you retain full rights and can sell the work again elsewhere.

Writing columns for a syndicate is rather different as they act as middle men, paying you directly and spending their time placing your work. They will take anything up to 50% of your fee for this service but save you time approaching publishers yourself. If you want wide exposure and have time to write regularly so that you have a high output, this can be a good way to earn a reasonable income; the syndicate may have far more contacts and a deeper knowledge of publishing outlets than you do.

COPYING AND ALCS

When it comes to pages from the books you have written, as well as articles, poems, scripts and other journal or magazine contributions, you will know all about copyright and that we are well protected from illegal copying in the UK by copyright laws. However, less well known is the fact that you can earn money every time someone makes a copy of anything you have written.

The body overseeing such payments is the Authors' Licensing and Collection Society (ALCS) which is based in London. It was set up in 1977 after pressure from the Writers' Action Group specifically to recoup revenue on behalf of writers for any use of their work. The money they collect in this way is referred to as secondary royalties and includes photocopying, scanning, digital reproduction and even cable TV, television programmes and repeat use of work on the Web.

You have to join ALCS to register your work and receive your payments as it is a body run by and for its members. Fortunately the one-off, lifetime fee is only about £25 and once you are a member you will receive the full amount that is due to you every year. The fee is actually deducted from your first payment so there are no up-front costs in joining.

ALCS is a large body with over 55,000 members and for the financial year 2010/ 2011 managed to pay out over £25 million. There is no limit on earnings and so payments to some authors can reach as high as £50,000 or £60,000.

There are two payment months each year – August and February – and to receive your money once you have joined you need to register your work at www.alcs.co.uk . If your books are already registered for PLR (see later) you don't have to repeat the details as the various bodies work together and, in fact, ALCS collects international PLR fees. However, you will need to register all your articles, essays and scripts.

It can take a little time as there are a number of boxes to fill in including, where relevant, the ISSN number (similar to a book's ISBN number but used for series of books or other publications) and the word count. If you are a regular contributor to the same publication and your articles have roughly the same word count, there is also a facility to register them all at once.

As you can imagine, it is hard for ALCS to operate as statistics are not collected on copying in the same way as, say, library lending. So they work in a rather round-about fashion. One major source of funds is from businesses, schools, universities, libraries and other public bodies such as government departments who photocopy or scan books and articles and so have to pay a fee to the Copyright Licensing Agency (CLA). This body carries out random sampling so that where titles and authors can be identified, the money collected can be passed on to ALCS and distributed appropriately.

Many sources are unattributable and here the money is placed in a general top-up fund and distributed to all members across the relevant categories.

EXERCISE 20
1. *If you have not already done so, find out more about ALCS.*
2. *If you are already publishing material but have not joined ALCS yet, register and add details of your work.*

****

CH. 5

THE LETTERS PAGE

Being selected for the letters page is more than just a matter of luck and some well-written prose. If you are serious about achieving publication, you need to prepare as thoroughly as you would for an article.

Even though you won't earn a large amount of money for each letter - at most you will normally receive £5 or £10 for a standard letter in a magazine (newspapers rarely pay for letters) – sending off a number of well-targeted letters each week can provide a regular trickle of income. Sadly, many publications nowadays limit rewards to the 'star' letter only. This can be a very elusive prize but well worth aiming for.

Some of you may think that writing letters isn't worth bothering about if you want to be a proper non-fiction writer. But there are several very good reasons to try your hand at them. In particular:

- Most publications print less than 3% of all letters they receive, so being selected for publication means you have been identified as a good writer
- It is excellent practice for telling a story succinctly
- Letters can be a surprisingly effective source of comfort or inspiration to readers
- Some books are based on letter collections or are written in letter form, so the practice can be useful if you have a wider aim

WHAT GETS PUBLISHED

If you don't have a burning issue on which to write, but just want to get into print, it is best to concentrate on the types of letters that are published regularly. No matter what magazine or newspaper you decide to target, you will usually find letters that can be classified under one of the following eight categories:

1. In praise of either a specific article or the whole publication
2. Personal anecdotes, including humorous stories
3. Controversial views
4. Initiating a debate
5. Instructional
6. A response to an earlier letter or feature
7. Hints, tips and general advice
8. Celebrity or royal gossip

MAKING YOUR LETTERS STAND OUT

For any category you select you need to make sure your own letter is more likely to be published than any others. To do this, it not only has to be written clearly and concisely but must have an added feature or slant that other writers may not have thought of.

Here are a few examples of my own published letters in each of the categories, to show how that extra factor was added.

1. *What a wonderful magazine or article:* You are going to be competing with hundreds of other writers all wanting to see their name in print, so you need an angle. If you are just praising, it adds nothing, so try to include an extra fact, supporting evidence of following it up or alternative point of view related to the item you read.

    I had one letter on this topic printed by a boating magazine because I started:

"My husband is a keen boat-owner but, dare I admit it, I have never taken to sailing. So I am amazed to find how much I enjoy reading his copies of... "

I then went on to say which aspects of their magazine I found interesting and why. They published it because a dislike of sailing was not a view likely to be duplicated by many other readers.

2. *Personal anecdotes*. If you want yours to be published, one option is to try including something helpful for readers, rather than just providing details of your own experience.

Advice. My letter describing the theft of my mother's handbag in a local supermarket ended with five practical tips on how elderly shoppers could keep their bags safe when using a shopping trolley.

Discovery. I won the star prize for a letter about complaints to retailers as I had discovered that companies don't read their own website feedback – only proper complaints in writing. I pointed out how short-sighted they were in not using this free source of valuable market research and warned readers to write in rather than just comment on a forum.

Best practice. In some cases, of course, a personal view on its own is welcome. This is certainly the case when the publication is running some type of campaign or working through a particular theme, as related anecdotes re-enforce the topic. That is why my experience (mentioned earlier in this book) as a trainee teacher trying to 'tell' rather than 'read' a story to 7-year-olds was published by an educational publication, as storytelling was a current issue and my experience was adding to 'best practice'.

Jokes or funny incidents. Although I haven't written one myself, a letter containing an overheard joke, a child's funny misunderstanding, a pet's antics or an example of a "senior moment" can lighten any letters page and so is usually welcome.

3. *Controversial views*. Here you need to moderate your tone if the subject makes you angry – no editor will publish a mad 'rant' – and phrase it in a way that is likely to encourage a response or at least strike a chord with readers.

At the time when there was a discussion going on about fining parents who take their children away from school during the holidays, a (tongue-in-cheek) letter I wrote was published because I set out reasons why it should be schools that are fined: for wasting teaching time with early end-of-term closures or half days off before a parents' evening, or by showing videos instead of working to the end of the year.

I wrote a letter for the *Times Higher Educational Supplement* containing advice about how universities could improve the experience of students starting university by abandoning the usual Freshers' Weeks format. It was published because it was related to "binge drinking", a topic in the news at the time.

4. *Initiating a debate.* You can pick practically anything for this sort of letter, as editors like topics that will encourage reader-response. A typical approach is to ask a question and solicit replies from readers. A computer magazine printed one of my letters asking what readers' thought was the right age for teenagers to be left unsupervised with the Internet. The local paper printed another complaining about new speed limits on local roads which were being ignored, as this generated several replies expressing different points of view.

5. *Instructional.* This type of letter is normally most common in publications strong on craft, cooking, gardening or technical content. So, for example, for a craft magazine I was selected for the star prize for a photograph and details of how I made a belt decoration in the form of strings of beads. As the magazine constantly received letters of this type, the main reason mine was chosen was because there was a celebrity link – the beads were copies of those worn by Johnny Depp in the Pirate films. (Although they published their own version of a copyright-free photo of the star, in my emailed letter I directed the editor to a relevant web page image just to show her how Mr Depp's decorations compared with mine.)

A more substantial letter that won the star prize was rather different. In it, I analysed seven factors that made a good small business. Not being in business myself, the letter was high risk, but I actually based it on watching a series of business "trouble-shooting" TV programmes. After a few of these, I could see the rules the trouble-shooter was following and so I set these out and sent the letter to a business magazine as a way to improve readers' management skills without them having to employ expensive consultants.

6. *In response to a previous topic:* Instead of just agreeing or disagreeing, you need to come up with a concrete suggestion or way of 'closing' the issue if it has run its course.

I won the star prize in a magazine by coming to the defence of non-technical parents told to be more vigilant when their children use Internet chat rooms. My letter explained why it was something that primary school teachers were in a better position to take responsibility for.

On a different note, another letter was published in a waterways magazine about a well-known canal side pub. In the previous issue, the editor had mentioned that canal closures had been fortuitous as their boat was very near to the pub and they could enjoy several visits. As I had had a terrible experience at the same pub, it was amusing to send them a letter to this effect, to counteract their praise.

7. *Hints, tips and advice.* As this is such a competitive field, you are more likely to have your advice published if you tie it in with products advertised in the publication or with relevant current concerns. Just 'another' chutney, stain removal or saved detergent story is unlikely to be interesting or different enough.

Advantage to the publication:: My letter suggesting growing houseplants from exotic fruit seeds and pips was published in a supermarket magazine because it linked three different aspects: saving money by growing your own plants; encouraging readers to buy more exotic fruit next time they went shopping; and fitting in with the "5 fruit or veg a day" campaign being championed by the supermarket.

Hot topic. Several years later, another contribution was published by the same magazine, but this time it was a recipe suggestion for how to deal with stale cake. As the publishers had just decided to add a "cut down on waste" column as a regular feature, this letter was very timely.

8. *Celebrity gossip.* Although similar to personal anecdotes, there is a particular place for celebrity or royalty news; name-dropping in the publishing world can open doors. I have yet to write one of these myself but if you can, your letter is very likely to be published.

As you can see, it is easier to get letters published if you take a basic idea and tweak it a little. Give it more value for readers, so that they gain useful information or advice, take a slightly different slant and make sure the publisher gains as well.

EXERCISE 21
1. *Select three or four different magazines, journals or newspapers that interest you and read the contributions carefully.*
2. *As you do so, see if any ideas for topics to write about come to mind, relevant to the different categories. For example: a funny quote (personal anecdote), advice on making something (instructional) or a disagreement with a voiced opinion (in response).*
3. *Jot them down and use them for later exercises. Hopefully you will end up with at least seven or eight different ideas for letters together with an appropriate target publication.*

LETTERS ABOUT THE PAST

If you have been thinking about or planning an autobiography, you may like the idea of making use of some of your personal memories to make a little money or at least get into print. When it comes to writing based around your past, there are certain types of letter that have a better chance of being selected for publication:

- Tips, hints or general advice related to handed-down recipes or things that our parents or grandparents did e.g. ways to save money, home remedies, solving gardening problems etc
- Reminiscence, particularly if accompanied by photographs e.g. showing the clothes you wore, places like old factories or schools, events such as fairs or holidays or work you carried out
- A humorous or embarrassing incident
- Links with well-known celebrities you once met or worked with
- Comparisons between how things are done now and what went on in the past, particularly if you select a topical subject
- How to do something you were an expert in

The best magazines to try with these types of letter are those covering history or genealogy or aimed at older readers in general such as *Saga, Choice, The Oldie* or *Yours.* You could also try general women's magazines. (Men often write these letters so don't be put off if you are not a woman!) An alternative is to find a magazine that publishes a regular page of readers' contributions such as "Weddings from the Past" or "Our Teenage Years."

Other publications may be more appropriate if the content of your letter relates to a specialist subject such as crafts, a regional slant, farming, waterways, TV programmes, parenting, boats, shopping, dieting, model-making, horses, music or vintage clothes. Local newspapers, although unlikely to pay, will usually be interested in stories from the past about the area or any change you can tell them about concerning buildings, workplaces, schools or amenities, especially if you have suitable photographs.

EXERCISE 22
1. *Using the ideas you came up with as you worked through this section, draft out some letters that would suit the publications you selected to concentrate on.*
2. *Can you find other publications that might be more suitable for some of the categories and draft some different letters?*

THE ACTUAL WRITING

You don't need to buy ten back copies and study the publication in great depth, but the clearer you are about the type of readers you are writing for, the more appropriate your letter is likely to be. So don't skimp on the analysis (see earlier) to discover the magazine's core readers and types of letter they particularly favour.

Whichever category you decide to write for, you will need to think carefully about style. As the same topic can be treated in a variety of ways, read the letters from two or three issues. If humour features strongly, have a go at writing your letter in the same vein. But if the magazine seems to prefer straight-forward advice with key points bulleted, make sure your letter will fit in with others on the page.

Keep the vocabulary appropriate, your writing clear and easy to read and the whole letter shorter than the maximum (worked out by checking the longest letter on the page). If your letter needs little or no adjustment, you won't provide the editor with a good reason to use someone else's contribution instead.

Particularly important when telling personal anecdotes – do not ramble and lose your reader in too many words. Have the point of your letter clear in your mind at all times and, if possible, ask a friend or relative to read through your finished letter and confirm that your point is expressed clearly enough. The major mistake most people make is to believe that all the facts and figures are necessary. They are not. What is necessary is to inform and entertain.

SENDING

Please note that nowadays, in practically all cases, letters are submitted in the form of emails as it is so easy to find a magazine or newspaper editor's email address or just the letters page contact. It is also a good way to send in any accompanying photographs, usually as jpeg thumbnails to start with to show what the finished photo will look like. (See later for further information on taking photos for print publications.) Send your letter in the main body of the message, not as an attachment as it should be short enough to be read comfortably and some editors don't like opening attached files.

When you email or write to the editor, don't forget to include your name, full postal address and telephone number. They may need to contact you and need to know where to send any payment.

ANONYMITY

In some cases, particularly letters containing personal anecdotes or involving a controversial issue, you may prefer to remain anonymous. If this is the case, make this point very clearly at the bottom of your message before you add your details. You will still need to provide these for the publication but they will then print your letter from: (*name and address supplied*).

EXERCISE 23

1. *If you are happy with any of the drafts you have created, find an appropriate publication to write to and check their letters page for style hints.*
2. *Write your letter up in an appropriate style and length for that publication.*
3. *Send it to the editor or letters page.*
4. *If the letter is not published and the topic is still current, find a similar publication and write to them instead. For example, if a letter is not accepted by "Amateur Gardening", try "Gardeners' World", "Kitchen Garden" or "Grow Your Own."*

CH. 6

ARTICLES

Just look through any magazine or journal, or the inside pages of most newspapers and you will find features on a wide range of topics. If you classify them according to type, they often fall into one of the following eleven categories and you may like to think about which categories you feel you could write for:

- Instructional, explaining to readers how to do something. This may be general e.g. ways to save time using your computer, or in clear steps with photographs – for example how to build a rabbit hutch.
- A round up of related topics e.g. 10 ways to treat a cough, or different methods for keeping your house warm
- Surveys carried out personally or a summary of a survey that has been made available to you
- Profiles or interviews of either an individual or several different people with something in common such as setting up their own business, working in the same organisation or having opposing viewpoints on a topic of interest
- An exposé using investigative journalistic skills to discover something such as the background to a controversial decision or development
- Human interest – this could be a confessional item, the inspirational story of someone who has overcome a disaster, disease or the death of a close relative or friend; an amazing adventure or feat, especially if performed by someone very old or very young; or a personal achievement

- Opinion pieces that can be your opinions or someone else's views on the world
- Humorous if you can write wittily about life
- Celebrity if you know, or are able to arrange to interview someone famous and can write about their life or their opinions, or if you used to know them before they were famous and can give readers an insight into their early life
- Informative - articles that provide straightforward information that can cover any topic from boating on the Kennet & Avon to Manchester's night life, superfoods or why teeth decay.
- Historical – either tracing the specific history of a place, family, building or organisation or more general e.g. the change from sheets to duvets or how we have taught reading over the past few decades.

EXERCISE 24

    1. Find two or three different examples of magazines, journals or newspapers.

    2. Go through and note down all the categories the articles fall into. Use the above classification or add new categories if the articles don't seem to fit any on the list.

RESEARCH

When you are ready to target a particular publication, it is a good idea first of all to look through some back copies. This way, you will see:

- What types of subject they do or don't cover, and if they have covered your proposed subject recently
- If you can spot any gaps that you could fill
- If you pick up ideas for similar articles you could write for a different publication

FINDING YOUR SUBJECT SLANT

To help narrow down the possible range of topics you could write about and give yourself more chance of having an article accepted, it is necessary to identify the most original approach you could take.

Once you have an idea for a main subject, there are many different ways to handle it and slant it for a particular readership. For example, if you wanted to write about weddings, there are so many possible approaches including:

- Being the mother or father of the bride – a personal view
- Organising a wedding (food, cake, flowers etc) – how to
- Dressing for the big day – informative or humorous
- Costs of a wedding – informative
- The job of a wedding planner – interview or profile
- Losing weight to get into the dress – how to, humorous
- Nearly missing your own wedding – personal story
- Places people can get married – round up
- How did he propose? – questionnaire/survey/interviews
- Local places people marry – local interest
- My wedding during the blitz – historical
- Running a wedding dress business – how to or interview

To generate ideas, particularly for more unusual or interesting aspects, it can sometimes work well if you create a spidergram. This is a method for generating new ideas related to an original topic by building up a "web" of related thoughts.

EXERCISE 25

1. *In Exercise 19 you started identifying specialist subjects or areas that you might be able to write about based on personal experience or interest.*

2. *Write down one of these topics - or any of the subjects covered by a magazine or journal that attracts you - in the centre of a blank piece of paper. (This is easier if*

you are away from the computer.) For example, you could write down Weddings or Canal boats.

3. *Allow your mind to wander and, as you think of any topic related to your main subject, e.g. wedding speeches or buying a narrowboat, write it down. Join it by a line to the central subject.*

4. *If that leads you on to a further, related idea, e.g. best man losing ring or selling a boat, link that by another line.*

5. *If no more ideas occur with that line of thought, return to the main subject and go off in a new direction e.g. wedding cake or canalside pubs.*

6. *You should end up with lots of different ideas related to the main subject, covering your paper like a spider's web. (Hence the name for the technique).*

7. *If you prefer lists, you can put your main subject at the top of the page and make different lists of related ideas as they come to you.*

Trying this exercise with the topic of Animals, I ended up with the following ideas:

- o Breeding
  - ▪ Certification/registration and the law
  - ▪ Showing
  - ▪ A day out at Crufts
  - ▪ Local event – preparing and winning
- o Accidents
- o Phobias
- o Sanctuaries
- o Pests
  - ▪ Loft
  - ▪ Kitchen
  - ▪ Dealing with a wasps' nest
- o The cost of pet illness & insurance
- o Pet businesses

- Dog walking
- Importing, collecting, breeding
- Boarding
  o Zoos
  o What to do when away on holiday
    - kennels and catteries
  o Farming
    - Vegetarianism
    - Slaughterhouses and abattoirs
    - Milk – historical picture
  o Training
    - Running a dog-training business
    - Taking a course with your pet (humorous)
  o Pet catchers
    - Battersea Dogs' Home
  o Children/old people
    - What it's like without a pet in the house
    - Dealing with death
  o Pets that go blind
    - guide dogs for the blind
  o Bites
    - Dangerous dogs – law
    - Dog fighting
  o Dog handlers e.g. police, immigration officers
    - Finding drugs

Once you identify one or more detailed topics you would like to write about, you can analyse them further until you have the particular story for your article. For example, taking the topic of "Dog fighting", you could look at the situation today – the people and dog breeds involved - or through history, films or books featuring dog fighting or even take a geographical view e.g. dog fighting in London, America or Asia.

If you prefer to expand on your ideas as you carry out the exercise, the subject of *Herbs*, for example, could result in the following:

- a list of all culinary herbs and how they are used
- a list of medicinal herbs and how they are used
- which herbs can be grown in the UK
- Making your own herb garden – the essential varieties and planting tips
- Herb gardens in Tudor times compared to today
- Herbs that only grow in certain countries e.g. the Mediterranean or the Far East
- Are there any historical events or characters linked to herbs e.g. sudden death, witchcraft etc?
- Which herbs are used in homeopathy?
- Do any herbs feature in Shakespeare or classic novels?
- Are there any specialist herb growers or suppliers to visit?
- Are there any books concentrating on herbs that could be reviewed?
- Herbs in song lyrics

LOCAL ANGLE

To write articles that will be published in local newspapers and magazines, you need to look at your area and community with fresh eyes. The ideal is to find people with personal views on topical events such as shopkeepers worried about a new supermarket; environmentalists concerned about the planned development of the river or beach; or parents involved in setting up a free school.

If you want to write a less time-dependent article, any of the above eleven types of magazine article can be given a local angle. For example, you may be able to write about a new group or club that has just been set up, perhaps interviewing members or organisers, or take a historical approach to a local organisation that will be celebrating its 10th, 25th or 50th anniversary. There may be special events or competitions that you could describe to readers, particularly if they are unique such as a music festival, cheese-rolling, pooh stick races or dragon boat racing; or you may be aware of an unusual beauty spot; a new business such as an English vineyard or cheese maker. You could retell a local ghost story or tale about a pub where a murder took place – especially if there is some topical connection you could make - or find someone well-known living locally whom you could profile.

If you enjoy the idea of developing local interest writing, it is worth cultivating contacts locally so that you have a number of people to call on for quotations or stories. Use local networking groups or online social media to build up your contacts.

EXERCISE 26
1. *Try to find a topic of local interest that you could write about.*
2. *Plan out an article.*
3. *Identify one or two publications that might be interested in your idea.*
4. *Research the newspaper or magazine carefully to check that this subject and your proposed treatment are suitable and the topic hasn't already been covered*

FILLING A REGULAR SLOT

Often finding a topic to write about is made easier by the publishers themselves. It is extremely common for magazines and journals to print a regular column with a set theme that needs to be filled every week or month with appropriate articles sent in by readers. If you have experience or can dream up a story or funny incident that fits the theme, you have a far better chance of getting it published than if you send the same 'orphaned' article in cold.

EXAMPLE
Readers Digest magazine say they pay: "£100 for true stories, jokes and other material we print in "It's Your Own Time You're Wasting", "Laughter" and "My Story".
An article about setting up my own craft club was published in Yours magazine for their regular "Follow Your Dream" column and another on setting up a ukulele club was going to appear in the same column but was published on their website instead.

You need to read a few back copies of the column to see the way the topics are handled and what has already been covered. For Readers Digest, for example, find copies online at http://www.readersdigest.co.uk/archive/past-issues-of-readers-digest.html

QUESTIONNAIRES

Near Christmas time or in the summer editions, magazines often go light-hearted and include an extra type of article such as a questionnaire; you can devise an amusing example of this type of article on almost any topic. As well as writing the questions, you need to prepare three or four summaries e.g. for those who answer mostly question As, question Bs or question Cs. You can keep it very silly or put in some more serious questions, for example related to looking after animals or children or dealing with personal relationships. You can also slant the content to cover any specialist topic you like.

EXAMPLE

For a gardening magazine, you could devise a quiz based on gardening habits e.g. "At the end of the summer, do you: A: plan next year's garden in detail B: just repeat what grew well or C: forget about things until spring?" The final summaries would, of course, comment on good and bad practice and give some useful advice.

RE-USING ARTICLE MATERIAL

Having created an article for one market, or – even better – before you carry out the preliminary research into a particular specialist area, it is worth thinking how you could angle your planned article for a different market. Do this instead of putting all your papers in a drawer marked "finished with" and you can double or treble your income from almost the same investment of time and effort.

For example, if you were making a study of the Modern Ambulance Service with the aim of getting an article published in "Ambulance

Today", you may be able to gather further information at the same time and use this for other articles along the following lines:

- an in-depth study of one or more ambulance services for local or regional newspapers
- a profile of a paramedic for a careers or training magazine or one aimed at teenagers
- a look at the changing uniform over the decades, or how the ambulance service started, for a historical journal
- interviews with drivers about their vehicles for a car or van magazine
- how paramedics compare to other scientific or medical workers - aim at careers or lifestyle magazines e.g. those published by The Sunday Times or Observer

If you find it hard to expand your possible options, ask yourself questions about the subject of your original article and analyse it in depth. This is likely to provide a number of leads you could then follow up. Either create a spidergram as in Exercise 25 or just do this as a brainstorm or list-making activity.

EXAMPLE
If you are writing about an organisation or company you may get article ideas if you ask questions such as:

- *Who are all the individuals or what are the different positions available?*
- *What is the organisational structure?*
- *How do you get in and how do you progress?*
- *What is the line of command?*
- *Are there any political, economic, social, environmental, scientific or artistic connections or implications?*
- *Is anyone famous linked to this organisation?*
- *Are there any international angles?*
- *Are there costs, salary or other financial factors worth pursuing?*

- *How has it changed over time?*
- *Is it expanding or contracting and why?*
- *Who could you interview and what would you want to learn?*

EXERCISE 27
1. *Take any topic you have written about or plan to do so.*
2. *Make as long a list as possible of alternative approaches to the same subject.*

ARTICLE STRUCTURE

Whatever type of article you decide to write, it is very important to plan the structure carefully. As there are potentially so many topics you could cover, you need to be selective and organise the material so that readers are steered through in a straightforward way. Rambling on, doubling back on yourself or going off at a tangent are all mistakes that could mean your article is rejected.

WHAT IS YOUR KEY MESSAGE?

Rather than sit down and try to write the introduction straight away, it is far better if you start by writing a very brief summary of exactly what the article will be about or what you want readers to get out of it. With that firmly in mind, you can then jot down all the topics you could cover on this theme. When you have more than you will need, prioritise and re-organise them into a satisfying plan. Cutting out topics that no longer fit the main theme is as important as including all salient points.

For example, if you have recently taken part in the Great North Run, your key message might be:

- you can take part in a run even if you are over 60 (so the article would raise issues concerning health and fitness at that age)

- here are some simple tips on training for your first run (so you would concentrate on the weeks and months before the race)
- learn how taking part in a run can be fun (you would provide information about all the fun things that happen on the day)
- how to raise money for charity by taking part in a run (you would provide information on sponsorship, how the money is raised, which charities could benefit etc)

EXERCISE 28

1. *Take any topic.*
2. *Summarise your message or line of argument so it is clear in your mind.*
3. *Spend 5 – 10 minutes coming up with as many ideas as possible related to this message.*
4. *Now cut these down to seven or eight and put them in a logical order.*

TITLES

You will hopefully have a title in mind, either right at the start or as your article starts to take shape on paper, but don't become too fond of it. Instead, you need to remember that this is just the working title. This is because, if the editor doesn't like it, he or she may want to use their own version. Of course, if you are clever, your title will be the best and only possible one that could be used, and so spending a little time thinking up a good title is well worthwhile. Here are a few ideas to help you think up suitable article titles. You can use the same ideas for book titles, chapter or even paragraph headings:

1. An apposite quotation taken from somewhere in the article
2. Straight forward description that tells readers exactly what is in the article e.g. *A Train Journey Through Cornwall*
3. Quotations from the Bible, Shakespeare or other well-known sources e.g. *Out Damned Spot* – an article about stain removal

4. Titles of poems, hymns, nursery rhymes, pop songs or carols e.g. *Silent Night* – on the subject of crying babies

5. Sayings and proverbs e.g. *Spare the Rod* (and Spoil the Child) – a feature about corporal punishment

6. A pun or play on words, perhaps rewriting one of the well-known quotes or titles e.g. *Sing a Song of 6p* (instead of sixpence) - a historical look at what your money could buy in the 50s compared to now

7. A quotation from someone you are profiling or interviewing

8. Catch phrases from TV, radio etc. For example Basil Fawlty's phrase: "*He's from Barcelona*" could introduce a travel piece

9. Proper nouns such as people's names, towns, the seasons, items of food etc. e.g. "*Little Weed*" (a character from the children's television programme "Watch with Mother") for a gardening article

10. Numbers – for articles that include a round-up of topics

11. Alliteration (each word starting with the same sound or letter) e.g. "*Magnificent Moving Machines*" – on diggers

12. Dramatic titles such as "*Help!*" or "*Lost at Sea*"

13. Spoonerisms (turning words round) e.g. "*Roaring with Pain*" (instead of pouring with rain)

EXAMPLE

Here are just a few article titles from a random selection of magazines:

- "*The Comeback Kids*"- about child stars and their current roles
- "*Shades of the Seventies*" – about sunglasses like those worn by Jackie Onassis
- "*Ten Ways to Stick to your New Year Resolutions*"
- "*Expert Guide to Lighting Your Home*"
- "*Chapter and Verse*" – profile of an author
- "*Animal Magic*" – cutting the cost of pet ownership
- "*Hair today, gone tomorrow*" – hair removal
- "*6 things you need to know about skin cancer*"

EXERCISE 29

1. *Take the subject of any article you might write and where you are clear about the message it will convey.*
2. *Think up five or six possible titles, using some of the ideas set out above.*

Note: take care not to use a quotation or well-known saying that doesn't fit the subject matter or message, just because you like the sound of it!

PUTTING THINGS IN ORDER

In most cases, a good article will have a beginning that is interesting enough to make readers want to carry on reading, clearly set out main contents and a closing summary or conclusion.

Beginnings

To make sure readers read the whole article, you need to grab their attention or hook them in. Here are some real examples:

A question e.g. "Mums with disabled children have one constant fear – what will happen to their child when they are no longer able to cope?" The article looked at one such family who had chosen supported living.

A controversial statement e.g. "All diets work – initially." The article then explained why most diets fail to keep the pounds off, and how a new discovery might solve the problem

A general observation e.g. "There is something evocative and romantic about the sound of musical instruments from centuries past." This was an article about six early music instruments.

Scene-setting e.g. "Staring out of the window at the blanket of snow outside, Megan and Alice Bailey were bored." The article was all about a game the girls had invented and sold.

Dialogue or quotations e.g. "I asked the wife: "Would you like your shoes cleaned?" is how an article about National Service started.

After an initial hook, the remainder of the introduction will usually set the scene for what will follow.

EXAMPLE
When out boating, I noticed that many women were opening and closing lock gates, which are heavy, whilst their male partners steered the boat through. After talking to a few women I discovered it was because they were nervous at managing the boat on their own in a lock. The answer was to give them confidence by explaining a few of the basic and easily-mastered techniques they could use. My article was published in "Canals & Rivers" magazine under the title "Ladies Who Lock"(a play on the saying "ladies who lunch") and the opening sentence read: "Next time you watch a boat going through a lock, check who is heaving the gates shut or straining to wind up the paddles." (Observation)

Mistakes unsuccessful writers often make with beginnings include:

- Starting off with a question or observation but then straying off the point, so that the content doesn't provide any answers. You need to make sure you keep the aim of your article clearly in mind so that it is satisfying to read.

- Instead of grabbing readers' attention, they begin with too much unnecessary background so that the point of the article is not clear right at the start. There is therefore no incentive for readers to bother to read down several paragraphs to find out what the article is all about. (A common recommendation for new writers is to write their article then delete the first two paragraphs! Often, the real article starts at paragraph 3.)

Middles

Once people start reading, the rest of the article should explain the situation, answer the question, modify the controversial statement or set out the reasons for your observation and any solutions you are offering.

In most cases, the main body of the article needs to be set out clearly and so constructed that points follow one another in a logical sequence. You will find that short paragraphs with or without subheadings work well, rather than presenting the reader with long indigestible blocks of text. Other tricks like bulleted or numbered lists will also make reading or skimming easier.

EXAMPLE
An article on saving money on fuel bills had the following paragraph subheadings:

1. *Introduction* - describing recent increases in energy bills
2. *How to cut costs* – suggestion to check if your current supplier has a cheaper tariff or to try switching
3. *Check out the competition* – using switching websites
4. *Pay your way* – it is cheaper if you use direct debits
5. *Do you want a fixed price?* – the pros and cons of fixing
6. *Take your pick* – a look at companies other than the big six
7. *Avoid cold callers* – warning about responding to door to door salesmen
8. *Other help at hand* – organisations offering discounts or with advice on cutting back on fuel use
9. *Heating oil* – advice for those not on mains electricity and gas
10. *More information* – help for those without a computer

Endings

A satisfying finish could be a:

- conclusion you can draw
- connection with the starting point
- good joke or punchline
- summary of the main points in the article
- suggestion for what to do or where to go next.

EXAMPLE

An article in Saga magazine started: "A dip into the Old Testament is proof of the fact that late-life fatherhood is by no means a new phenomenon." (The hook)

Although this tells readers straight away that the article is about older fathers, it is confirmed by the rest of the introduction: "Abraham was 100 when Isaac was born and Isaac – like father like son – didn't sire Esau and Jacob until he was in his sixties.................Jacob, the book of Genesis tells us, loved Joseph more, simply because he was the son of his old age."

The article then switched to modern fathers and introduced 10 well-known men who had their children late in life. It ended with a quote from Warren Beatty about having four children and at each birth, when he moves down from being number one in the household to number two, three and then four he gets " more and more happy". The concluding sentence returned to the opening of the article by stating: "No doubt if Jacob had lived in the 21st century he would have said exactly the same thing."

EXERCISE 30

1. *Take a topic you have identified from earlier exercises that you could write about.*
2. *Plan an article for a publication you can clearly target.*
3. *State your key message.*
4. *Set out the 5 – 10 main points you want to make in the body of the article.*
5. *Is there a story in it to help you involve your readers more?*
6. *Check that you have a hook to attract readers, content that will provide an appropriate answer and a final summary or conclusion that draws the whole thing together.*
7. *Write the article.*

USING YOUR PLAN

Working as a non-fiction tutor, I have seen a number of outlines for articles together with the finished articles and find the same three mistakes are repeated over and over again:

1. No key message: Writers don't make an early decision about their main message and, without it, neither plan nor finished article can be successful. Readers are taken on a rambling tour of the topic and the message is lost.

2. Ignoring the plan: A good outline is thought through and laid out clearly but then the writers don't look at it again. If your plan is good, it is best to stick to it. To find out if you have made this mistake once you have written a first draft of your article, check every paragraph and summarise exactly what it is saying. Instead of imagining you have followed your plan, you will soon see whether you have completely changed the order of topics, included far too much unnecessary information and made it top heavy, or veered off the point you thought you were going to make. Once you have the actual list of paragraphs you have written in front of you, you can compare it to the plan and put things right very easily in a second draft.

3. Skimpy plan: Some plans are unclear and just jotted notes with no obvious logic or structure. To be of value, make sure you can clearly see the progression of the article through every paragraph.

EXERCISE 31

1. *Analyse every single paragraph in the article you wrote for Exercise 30.*
2. *Compare it to your plan, and check it against your key message.*
3. *Do you need to make any changes, perhaps to the balance of the article, the order of topics, to cut out sections or fill in any gaps?*

NON LINEAR ARTICLES

An alternative to a logical sequence of ideas is to group together a more random collection of topics.

If you are writing a round-up style article, these will be the equivalent of a list. For example an article about breeds of dog might have six or seven sections each devoted to one breed. Here, the paragraph headings will be the breed name.

If you are writing on a single subject, you need to select appropriate topics and then introduce them perhaps with quotations or even by employing a question and answer technique, turning the paragraphs into a series of answers to queries you set out as paragraph headings.

EXAMPLE

An article about Robert Vaughn in Yours magazine where there was no linear organisation of topics had the following quotations from the star as paragraph headings:
"I don't take fame too seriously"
"You don't feel fear when you're young"
"Work keeps you young"
"Family life is important to me"
"Parties aren't my scene"
"English history fascinates me"

WORD COUNT

When an editor agrees to take your article, they will normally let you know how long it should be as well as any other requirements.

EXAMPLE

Here is an email I received from one editor accepting an article: " I envisage that the feature could be around two to three pages, so the wordage would be around 1500 with around six to eight images (jpegs if possible, please), captioned."

You need to stay as close to the word count as you possibly can; it is usually very important for fitting the right number of articles and advertisements into the publication and editors don't want to have to do the work themselves.

EXERCISE 32
1. *Take any article topic and write the introduction or a main paragraph that is around 120 - 140 words long.*
2. *Now rewrite it so that it is exactly 90 words long without losing any of the sense.*
3. *Decide if you have improved the writing or not. (If you have to cut an article for real, you need to be sure the cuts improve rather than ruin the writing.)*

SIDE BARS

Look at any article and you will often find a separate short item on the same page, perhaps set out as bulleted points against a coloured or shaded background that is associated with the feature but is still clearly separate. This is known as a side bar and usually offers readers extra information that doesn't fit into the main body of the text. It can take a number of different forms including:

- Case studies
- Sources of further information or help e.g. books, websites or organisations including their contact details
- Suppliers of goods mentioned
- Expert views or quotations
- A summary of relevant points
- Relevant tips
- DIY advice

When preparing your article, it can be a good use of time to think about what could be added to give readers extra information or help. If appropriate, either include this with your finished article or mention what you have in mind and tell the editor that it could be provided before any deadline.

EXAMPLE

An article in Prima magazine was a personal account by someone with Reflex Sympathetic Dystrophy. The side bar explained what RSD was, how to diagnose yourself and alternative treatments available.

In Your Home magazine someone had written about their home and the article included a number of photographs. The bedroom showed a suspended bed and a side bar explained how to build one.

An article in Yours magazine about the horse trainer Jan Vokes had a side bar detailing three different films starring horses.

EDITING AND PROOF READING

If you've ever received a letter or email that contains grammatical or spelling mistakes, or read a book that had chunks of text missing or in the wrong places, you know how irritating it can be. A professional image is even more important when you are trying to impress an editor.

It goes without saying that ALL work should be typed. Not only because nowadays so much material is sent electronically but even when sending articles by post, editors will expect (normally double-spaced) typed manuscripts that they can read easily.

There are two aspects to checking manuscripts:

1. Making sure there are no basic errors such as grammar, punctuation or spelling mistakes that are normally (but not always) picked up by computer software built into word processing packages like Microsoft Word. Take particular care with:
   - Singulars instead of plurals or vice versa
   - Repeated words or sentences
   - Transposed letters where the words are nonsense but still spelled correctly and so not picked up by a spell checker e.g. *meat* instead of *team*.

2. Reading for sense. This will pick up more subtle errors like:
    - The whole piece not hanging together properly
    - Long-winded or rambling prose
    - Badly worded text
    - A change of tense mid-way through
    - Chunks of text (often those cut and pasted or copied across) in the wrong place

DRAFTING

Rather like being drunk, your words can seem absolutely brilliant when you write the last sentence and finally put down your pen or take your hands off the keyboard. Sadly, you can be too close to your own writing and no manuscript, however short, should be sent off immediately. Instead, regard this original piece of writing as a first draft and never as the finished work.

Leave your work for a few hours or days and then read it through again. As well as checking every comma and full stop, this distance will allow you to see it more clearly and you may well discover that there are several places where you have worded things badly or it becomes clear that you have not got your point across well enough. As long as you give yourself time to rewrite, and are prepared to do this several times, redrafting is the only way to end up with work of the highest standard.

PUNCTUATION

There are five major errors that even well-educated and qualified writers can make, so you may like to check that you don't have a problem with any of these:

Apostrophes

There are only two places where you use an apostrophe:

1. To represent a missing letter:
Instead of writing "you are" you can write "you're"

Instead of writing "cannot" or "do not" you can write "can't" or "don't" Instead of writing "it is" or "there is" you can write "it's" or "there's"

2. To show possession:
Where one person owns one or more items, you show this by putting the apostrophe after the singular form
E.g. a **boy** has a cat, so it is the **boy's** cat, or
A **child** has five toys, they are the **child's** toys, or
Janet has some exams so they are **Janet's** exams

Where more than one person share or own one or more items, you put the apostrophe after the plural form
E.g. two girls share a car, so it is the **girls'** car, or
Several men own a business, so it is the **men's** business, or
Two neighbours both have allotments, so they are the **neighbours'** allotments

Apostrophes are never used where the word is simply a plural
E.g. "I have seven **bananas**"

They are also never used where the word is a possessive pronoun
E.g. If the ball belongs to you it is **yours**, or
If the ball belongs to the dog it is **its** ball, or
If the house belongs to a couple, it is **theirs**, or
If the books belong to her they are **hers**

Colons

There are three different places where you can use a colon, (although you could also reword your text if you don't like using them). In all cases, it seems to act as a natural pause, giving the sense that something must now follow:
a. At the start of a list
I need to buy three things: paint, a paintbrush and some wallpaper paste.
(Or: I need to buy paint, a paintbrush and some wallpaper paste.)

b. To introduce dialogue or a quotation
As it says in Hamlet: "To be, or not to be"
(Or: The quote "To be or not to be" comes from Hamlet.)
c. To answer a question, resolve an issue or add emphasis when completing a statement

There is only one thing that will work: I'll have to marry her.
(Or: The only thing to do that will work is to marry her.)

Semi-colons

There are two different ways to use a semi-colon:

1. Between list items when the text is too complex and would otherwise have too many commas and become confusing:
    "I had bacon, eggs, tomatoes and fried bread for breakfast"
    But
    I had two rashers of crispy, fried bacon; two eggs lightly poached; some tomatoes I picked that morning in the garden; and some of mother's homemade bread, fried lightly in butter.

2. Where you might have written two short sentences that have something in common or that are contrasting, you may prefer to join them with a semi-colon to make a single, more complex sentence.
    The morning was hot; by the afternoon it had started to rain.
    Or
    I was really tired; I stayed in bed all day.
    (The alternative is to join the two sentences with a comma and then a word like "while", "but" or "so" e.g. I was really tired, so I stayed in bed all day.)

Commas

As you have seen, commas are used to separate a number of simple items or ideas, to combine with a joining word to join two short sentences or, in pairs, to cut off a less important part of a sentence.

Reading your work aloud can usually indicate where a comma might be needed.

- *Lists* e.g. I like fruit, chocolate, nuts and crisps. (Note that a comma is not usually needed before the final "and". If used, it is known as an Oxford comma and it can be helpful if the final item is complex. For example: "I cut off the red and white braid, blue and yellow buttons, and yellow and green striped sleeves".)
- *Joining* e.g. Come over on Friday, or I won't be able to see you again.
- *Pairing* e.g. When the train arrived, after a long delay, I rushed to find a seat.

Sentences and new paragraphs

Again, by reading aloud it is usually fairly obvious when a new sentence needs to be started, and if you have trouble with sentence structure you probably need to buy a good grammar book.

One mistake writers can make is to lose sight of the reader and to write far too much as a single block of text. Even if no new point is made as such, think about starting a new paragraph rather than write too much and create single large blocks of text that might put readers off. There is no rule as to how many sentences any paragraph should contain, but if you make a new point you should normally start a new paragraph.

POOR SPELLING

The advice to check your spelling is not much use if you don't believe or cannot tell when you have made a mistake, so if in the past you have had trouble with spelling:

- Always use the spell checker on your computer and use a dictionary if a range of unrecognisable spellings is offered to you

- Ask other people to read through your work, in case they can spot spelling mistakes or words used incorrectly (e.g. *their* instead of *there*, *practise* instead of *practice* etc)

- Use a dictionary for any words you are not absolutely certain of, even if they are not picked up by the computer

EXERCISE 33

Correct all the errors you can find in the following article:

After holidaying in Barcelona we left our hotel to get to the airport, several hours early. To leave time for lunch and some final shopping our hotel had been picked for its location; so all we had to do was wheel our cases round the corner and catch one of the frequent airport buses.

Bag checks done, boarding passes in hand, we found ourselves on a mezzanine floor; overlooking a large shopping mall. Down below restaurants; shops; and coffee bars where spread out before us. And our main problem would be: deciding where to eat. Above our heads was a large notice with an arrow pointing to our boarding gate and nothing else visible except an unmarked escalator, a scrolling advertising screen and the passport checkpoint manned by a smiling officer. Passport checks took a few second and we were now through, ready to make our way down to the treasure's below. We wander along the concourse both left and right, but could only find one down escalator clearly marked "Toilets Only". So we stopped a passing stewardess to ask her how to reach the shops.

"You have past passport control," she said, and made to walk off.
I stopped her with a light hand on her sleeve.
"Yes, that's right. So how do we get to the shops?"
"No," she said. Severely: "you have come through passport control. You cannot go there." And this time I let her go.

Non comprendo, I thought to myself, although her English it was perfect. There was clearly a communication problem so we found a cleaner. His English was poor, but understandable.
"You come through here. You cannot go there."
Finally, in the small gift shop I was given a fuller explanation.
"Didn't you see the notice," asked the saleswoman.
"What notice?"

Just then, we heard an English voice asking someone in the shop how they could get downstairs to the restaurants. So we weren't the only idiot tourist to miss this large notice.

"The large green notice by passport control. It says once you have your passport checked you cannot return you cannot return."

Well, excuse me but there was no notice. Just a scrolling advertising board we hardly glanced at. Was that it?

TRAVEL PIECES

Travel writing is seen as somehow different, compared to other types of magazine or newspaper article writing. But even if you specialise in travel writing, you will have to follow very similar rules if you want to be successful. So you still need to identify your readership, provide a hook to encourage readers to stay with you and decide how to treat your topic.

There are a number of different types of travel writing. You could emphasise:

- information
- humour
- opinion
- nostalgia
- 'how to', or
- combine several of these

TRAVEL REVIEWS

One common approach is to write a review. This needs to be helpful to people thinking of taking a similar trip and so must include everything they will require to make sensible choices. Usually this means good quality advice based on factual information setting out the pros and cons of visiting a particular place, using certain travel companies or spending money on any extras such as tickets, car hire or guides that may be offered to them. As with all other types of article, understanding the readers is vital for a travel writer as a piece aimed at young families or teenagers, for example, will be very different to one targeting retired couples.

There are now many websites providing free travel reviews, the most well known being Trip Adviser and Silver Trip Adviser, and so your review for a magazine must be different and better than these. As they are usually fairly formulaic (rating accommodation, food and transport etc) there is still lots of scope for an individual approach.

One possibility is to write a review that could be marketed to a local newspaper or magazine. If you have a small regional airport you could concentrate on just those countries and cities local people can fly to. As well as countries to visit, you could also write about the airlines that use the airport, the facilities or the costs and difficulties of getting to the departure lounge or even about the on-site cafes and restaurants - aspects of most relevance to local people.

SENSE OF PLACE

If you want to write evocative, impressionist pieces, the main thing that distinguishes good travel writing from the ordinary is that it offers an exceptional sense of place. Readers don't enjoy being made jealous by writers boasting about the hotels, trips or food they have enjoyed, often on expenses, but instead will hope to be enthralled, excited and inspired by the wonderful people and places that you conjure up for them. Your article needs to convey to readers the flavours (smells, tastes, sounds, feel) of the place, the customs, the unusual people they could meet, the difficulties they may face but that can be overcome, and the pleasures that await them. It also needs to be up-to-date, especially if you are giving currency, health, safety or other advice.

These articles especially demand the best of fiction-writing skills such as having a story to tell, employing all the senses, adding in small details and including some dialogue, to make sure readers experience the place along with you. You may be providing photos as well, but never rely on them to tell your story.

EXAMPLE

Many people want to write travel pieces, so here is what Hidden Europe magazine look for:

"Only very rarely do we accept travelogues, and we have never published a simple account of a writer's holiday, no matter how exotic the destination. We are looking for something more: a wide and balanced understanding of how a place and its people function, backed up by reasoned views, careful explanation and perceptive insights. These are not the sort of properties easily born of just a brief engagement with a destination. We like what we publish to reveal the authority that the author brings to the topic. Where we contract external authors, we really are looking for something that is evocative, impeccably researched and well crafted. Our external authors have often lived and worked in the areas about which they write."

EXERCISE 34

You are going to write a travel piece suitable for the Daily Telegraph's "Just Back" competition.

1. *Visit the website at www.telegraph.co.uk/travel/travel-writing-competition/ and read some of the winning entries to get an idea of what they are looking for*

2. *Either think back to a trip you have taken in the past or use a recent journey for your article. If you haven't travelled anywhere for some time, spend an hour or so walking round your local town or village and imagine being a tourist who is visiting for the first time.*

3. *Write a travel article in under 500 words that tells a story and has a strong sense of place.*

4. *If the competition is still running and you feel your article is a possible winner, enter by sending your work in the body of an email message to justback@telegraph.co.uk and include your contact details.*

PHOTOGRAPHS FOR MAGAZINES

Nowadays, it is usual to supply photographs with your article, rather than expect the editor to source these for you. After looking at other articles in the publication you will get a sense of how many and what types of photograph are required and can send thumbnails of those you are hoping to use. If you have not yet written the piece or need to make a special journey or spend money before you can take the photos, you should mention that photographs will be provided if and when your article idea is accepted.

When you provide photos, you should also write a short caption for each one. This text is usually displayed on top of or alongside the pictures.

Print publications prefer to receive jpeg or tiff digital images. When you are taking pictures that will be printed there are three dimensions to worry about: file size, image size and resolution (dots per inch). File size is the amount of hard disc space a compressed image will occupy measured in megabytes (Mb) whereas image size relates to the number of dots or pixels in the image (see table below). You may see resolution measured in megapixels e.g. 2MP or 3MP which means the image contains 2 or 3 million pixels. Reasonably priced digital cameras nowadays can often take 12MP or 14MP pictures.

As the number of pixels increases, so does the resolution or clarity of the image. The two standard measures for resolution are dots per inch (dpi) and pixels per inch (ppi). In printing and publishing, the standard threshold for image clarity is 300 dpi so you should never take your pictures at lower than 300 dpi and the best practice is to take them at as high a resolution as you can without making the photo file too big to send. This will allow the publishers to enlarge your photo as much as they want to without losing any clarity or getting "blocky" images. A full page A4 picture (roughly 11.5" x 8.5"), for example, would need to be approximately 3600 pixels high by 2500 wide (9MP).

If you want to send images by e-mail for a magazine editor to view, send small, fast-loading thumbnails e.g. 640x480 resolution and explain that they are not the finished item. You can then send the full images on a CD. A blank CD can hold about 600Mb of images which is 120 images at 5Mb in size.

Resolution	Size (MB)		Print size	
	2".3"	4".6"	5"7"	8"x10"
640x480 (0.3MP)	0.14 Excellent	Good	Poor	Poor
800x600	Photo quality	V Good	Reasonable	Poor
1280x960 (1MP)	0.45 Photo Quality	Photo	Very good	Good
1600x1200(2MP)	0.9 Photo Quality	Photo	Photo Quality	V.Good
2048x1536(3MP)	1.35 Photo Quality	Photo	Photo Quality	Photo
3072x2034(7MP)	3.15 Photo Quality	Photo	Photo Quality	Photo
3264x2448(8MP)	3.5 Photo Quality	Photo	Photo Quality	Photo

EXERCISE 35

1. *Do you have a camera or mobile phone that takes pictures at a resolution of 3MP or higher? If not and you want to write articles for magazines – is it time to think about buying one?*

2. *If you have one – do you know how to download the photos onto your computer? If not, it is time to get out the manual or follow any on-screen instructions.*

3. *Take and find a photo and check its properties. If you have not done so before but have photo-imaging software, learn how to manipulate your images e.g. cropping to remove unwanted objects.*

WHY ARTICLES ARE REJECTED

No writer has everything they write, or all their ideas for articles, actually accepted, and so you must expect rejections now and again. (If nearly everything is rejected, you clearly have a serious problem, but hopefully that won't happen after you have read this book and taken note of the advice.)

There are many reasons why contributions from established writers, let alone novices are rejected, but here are five that you may be able to do something about:

1. The idea for an article arrives at the wrong time. For example, the publication may have recently covered the same topic or has plans to do so already in place. This is just bad luck and the best thing to do is target it elsewhere.

2. The editor doesn't think the idea will work for them. This may be because you didn't analyse the publication or readership carefully enough or it is simply a personal view. In such cases you could possibly rewrite it and pitch again (but this is rather a long shot, once it has been rejected) or target it more carefully elsewhere.

3. Your piece is poorly written, perhaps in stilted prose with the overuse of generalisations or cliches, badly organised, containing too many facts and figures or wandering off the point. In these cases, it is a question of working on your

writing skills (see Chapter 3) and improving the overall organisational structure.

4. The article is written in the wrong style for that publication or readership. This is definitely a case of not doing your homework and, if you are going to send it to a different publication, make sure you analyse the types of article they publish very carefully first.

5. It contains too many grammatical or spelling mistakes. This is easily put right if you carry out careful editing and proof reading. Ask someone else to check the finished work if you have always had problems with your English.

EXAMPLE

As an example of the second reason, I suggested an article idea on Public Lending Right and ALCS to a well-known writing magazine. The editor rejected it as: "it is something we have covered before and I think it is best to mention it in passing in other articles or regular features." On the other hand, Writing Magazine liked the idea and it was published in March 2012 as a stand-alone article with the title "Earning Money from Writing".

QUERY LETTERS

Magazines, journals and newspapers used to prefer to receive a letter or email suggestion for a contribution rather than a full manuscript because:

- they wouldn't have time to read through all the submissions in full, especially as many will be complete non-starters
- they may like the basic idea but would prefer a different format, length, target audience or type of contribution and there would be less room for manoeuvre if you simply presented the finished piece

However, a quick search on the Internet shows that many are now quite happy to receive a full article, and often as an attachment. So the best advice is – read their submission guidelines and follow every point!

To give your idea the best possible chance of being adopted, where they don't want the finished piece, you need to send in your suggestion in the form of a well-reasoned query letter or email. A good way to understand the process is to imagine yourself as an editor.

EXERCISE 36
1. *You have just started publishing a monthly newsletter about your own town and someone you know nothing about has written asking if you would like to publish an article they propose writing on the town's history.*
2. *Jot down five things they could say or do that would convince you to take their idea further.*

CONTENTS

When doing the above exercise, you have probably thought of some of the following questions they would need to answer:

- Can they write and would their writing be in the style you publish?
- Are they knowledgeable enough about the topic?
- Would their item be interesting or entertaining enough for readers?
- Will it duplicate anything you published recently, or plan to publish soon?
- Do they have any publishing experience, to give you more confidence in their abilities?
- Are they reliable – would they deliver on time?

Providing the answers would require them to supply:
1. All or a sample of the piece itself, or some evidence of writing skills. If their original letter or email was badly

written and full of grammatical mistakes, it would not be a good start.

2. A CV or list of qualifications and experience that showed they knew their subject, or a good reason why they had the credentials to write this particular feature.

3. An outline of what their piece would cover. This would also confirm whether or not the approach would duplicate or complement other contributions.

4. A track record in writing/publishing – even writing reports, committee papers or song lyrics would be better than no experience at all

5. A date when the piece would be ready – especially if it involved time-consuming research.

Also important would be the reason why they want to contribute to your newsletter and what your readers would gain from the item. This would show that they had targeted their work appropriately and carried out the necessary analysis of your publication. It may also help persuade you to publish when you might otherwise have decided to reject the idea.

This exercise tells you what needs to go into a query letter:
- A summary of your idea
- why they are the right publication
- evidence that you can write and deliver
- your credentials for being the appropriate author

A note for email queries: remember that, although emails are usually more relaxed than letters, this is a business communication. Always write "Dear Ms Smith" or "Dear Jo Smith" rather than "Hi Jo".

REGULAR COLUMNS

The ideal for many writers is to be offered a regular slot in a publication. Each week or month, you know that you have a target to write for and will be paid for your contribution.

When it comes to opinion pieces, this is normally the province of a celebrity, staff member or well-known writer, but there are other options you may be able to suggest or be asked to write, usually based on previous one-off contributions or your particular expertise.

If you have an idea for a column and can find an appropriate magazine or website that doesn't publish it yet, there is no reason why you can't suggest writing for them. This is likely to be welcomed particularly by one of the lesser-known publications such as the trade or local press or new online magazine-style websites that are building up a core of readers and are often happy to go along with new ideas.

To pitch, you need to tell them:
1. What the publication would gain from such a column
2. Why it suits their particular readership
3. Why you are the best person to write it

STYLES OF REGULAR COLUMN
Here are some of the different styles of column you might write:

Question & Answer or Problem Pages (Agony Aunts)
These typically cover personal, financial, gardening, pets, nutrition, education, health, DIY or technical issues. Usually they provide answers to real queries sent in by readers, but if no-one sends in a question that you believe will appeal to a wide audience you will have to think up some questions yourself.

EXAMPLE
As an IT tutor and published author of a couple of computing books, I successfully pitched the idea for a computing Q & A column to two websites and one magazine, and my current column: You Can Do IT has been running on www.laterlife.com since 2004.

EXERCISE 37
1. Spend five minutes making a list of some of the areas of expertise you have on which you might offer specialist advice.

2. *When you identify a topic, try to find a similar Q & A column and read the examples to give you an idea of what is involved.*

3. *Think up one or two new questions and draft out possible answers.*

4. *Find some publishers you could approach with your ideas for a Q & A page.*

Diaries

A number of regular columns feature one person's experiences over time – either a week or for several months. These can range from trainee teachers to readers trying out a new diet, moving to the country or living with a disability. If you find the right topic and approach a relevant publication, it is quite likely that they would be interested in your story. One example of a writing diary was the *Diary of a Freelance Hack* published in Writer's Forum and others have included a week in the life of a trainee teacher published by the Times Higher Educational Supplement and a 10-week reader's fortnightly diary in *Yours* describing her successful weight loss.

EXERCISE 38

1. *Are you involved in any activities or jobs that you might be able to diarise?*

2. *If so, draft out a few examples of what you could write about.*

3. *Try to find a publisher who might be interested and think about selling them the idea.*

Round Ups

Bits and pieces of information can get lost if spread throughout a publication and so there are usually one or more pages in most magazines containing up-to-date news or features on a number of linked items.

It is often a good place for numbers e.g. "Five must-see exhibitions ...." "Ten top tips on..." or "Three things you should know about ...."

Examples include:

- What is coming up in your area – festivals, events, open gardens etc
- Different methods for ......
- What is new in the shops

Mini-Reviews

Although reviews of last night's TV or new films can take up an entire page, it is common to bring together a number of shorter reviews into a single column. These often cover items such as cookery or gardening books; household gadgets; new food or drink products such as sauces, jams or mixers; health remedies or cosmetics. Sometimes readers may be asked to review products and write a report, but often one writer will cover the range themselves.

One I discovered recently was a monthly look at different "collectables", which would be perfect for a writer with a strong interest in antiques. (For more on reviewing in general, see the next chapter.)

Recipes

As well as one-off contributions, you may be lucky and land a regular cookery column. For many years, a major newspaper ran a column featuring readers' recipes from the past where contributors had to send in the actual handwritten or typed recipe (or a photo of it) and tell the story behind the food. A twist on this sort of column or on a different but topical theme such as seasonal vegetables, dinners for one, meals in five minutes etc. would be very easy to create if you enjoy cooking, and it could be the start of a whole new career.

EXAMPLE
Even celebrity chefs have to start somewhere and you may not know that Delia Smith began her career in 1972 writing a regular cookery column for the London Evening Standard. She went on to write for

the Radio Times before bringing out her successful book "Frugal Food".

Themes

This is where a regular columnist can contribute a single article-like piece or combination of snippets of information, round-ups and how-to tips under a general heading such as "Garden Clippings" or "Creative Projects".

Interviews

These are an excellent way to bring bang up-to-date material to a paper or journal. For a regular column, you would need to run these under a theme such as: Local business people, Well-know local inhabitants or Unusual jobs.

Projects

If you have specialist knowledge, for example in plumbing, finance, the environment or gardening, you may be able to suggest six or eight related articles that could feature over several months. A column on energy saving, for example, could feature articles covering insulating the roof, boiler maintenance, draught proofing, cavity wall insulation and pipe lagging. Again, a gardening series on fruit trees could cover pruning, training, planting, grafting and storing produce.

EXAMPLE

In 2013 I approached a writing magazine with an idea for a one-off article on new writers' mistakes, and this was developed into a series of monthly articles called "Feature Fix".

EXERCISE 39

1. *Look through a number of different publications or online magazines and try to find examples of regular columns.*
2. *Take a note of any that you personally might be able to write.*

3. *Can you find, or think of an idea for a new column (apart from the diary or Q & A page you have already worked on) that might be marketable?*

4. *For all the columns you feel you would be happy to write, plan out and send off a query letter.*

****

CH. 7

FILLERS AND REVIEWS

Look through any magazine or journal and you will see a number of items that take up half or a quarter of a page or even less. These are known as "fillers" and do what they say – fill up empty spaces between longer pieces or at the bottom of a page.

One specialist area is reviewing and reviews can either act as short fillers or they can be expanded to become a complete article. Everyone knows what a review is, and hopefully you are realistic enough to discount landing the job as a national newspaper TV, restaurant or book reviewer when you have little or no background or experience in this field: this work is normally the pinnacle of any reviewer's ambitions. But there are more opportunities for freelance writers in the whole area of reviews than you might think.

FILLERS

Anything relevant to the publication's content can be used for a filler and it often helps if there is an accompanying photo. Content can be a mini-version of any subject that could be written as a full-blown article such as how to or celebrity gossip, but may also fall into one of the following categories:

- information on a scientific, historical, language, food or travel theme
- a recipe or unusual use for condiments or herbs
- puzzles, quizzes or crosswords
- heart-warming stories
- health, fitness or nutrition tips
- topical news of research or report findings
- humorous stories, press cuttings, misprints etc

- stories linked to special events, celebrations, bank holidays etc.

EXAMPLE
Readers Digest magazine pay "£60 for contributions to end-of-article fillers. Press cuttings and photos of funny signs or incidents are particularly welcome."

TYPES OF FILLER

Here is some guidance on writing fillers for the various categories listed above:

Information

If you know or can find out facts or figures that would be relevant, and can present them in an amusing or interesting way, short items of this sort could well be attractive to a relevant publication.

Openings for these items often take the form of:
- Did you know .....
- The discovery of the ....
- The first time...........
- Over the past twenty years, more than ....

EXAMPLE
"Yours" magazine once printed a column on "How we entertained... " in the 1970s, 1980s, 1990s and 2010, showing how tastes have changed in relation to favourite meals out and which TV chefs we like watching.

Recipes

In publications where the main emphasis is not food and drink, they often publish one-off recipes. These are perfect fillers as they can include photos of any size to take up more space or can be squeezed by setting out the ingredients in time-saving columns. Some magazines are food-based, but even these need contributions from readers and they are more likely to take a filler from an unknown writer than offer you an entire 2-page spread.

As always, it is important to have a story behind your recipe. Why should your cake, stew or ice-cream recipe be worth publishing? Give them a good reason and they are far more likely to publish.

EXAMPLE
Here is the text of a short email I sent with a recipe that resulted in my winning a case of wine from "Olive" magazine: "Your current issue shows a number of photographs of cheese and oatcakes, but these biscuits are quite expensive to buy. I bake my own which are not only delicious but also very quick and easy to make".

Puzzles and quizzes

Puzzles and games can be given any slant. For example, a recent filler published in a writing magazine consisted of a draft manuscript containing 20 proof-reading errors that readers had to identify and correct.

An "Out of Order" quiz is very easy to create – find several major events that most readers will know about, list them out of order and ask which year and in which order they took place. For example, in a quiz of this type for an over 50s magazine the topics included the landing on the moon, a well-known author winning the Nobel prize and the inaugural flight of a famous plane. For a sporting or literary magazine, you would pick more relevant or specialist events.

If you are a good photographer (although there isn't much writing involved!), you could even create a quiz based on picture clues such as flowers, birds, vegetables or kitchen utensils viewed from odd angles.

EXERCISE 40
1. Think of a named publication or category such as home-making, cooking, television or the countryside. Newspapers often have puzzle and game pages so don't forget these.

2. *Think of an appropriate topic that could form the basis for a quiz or short activity and draft it out to fill ¼ page.*

3. *If you think it is marketable, write it up carefully and send it to the editor of a relevant publication.*

Heart warming stories – or the opposite

Editors like uplifting stories and, I am afraid, many also like scandals and real-life horror stories, so personal anecdotes of either type may find a market.

If we concentrate on the more positive ones, the ideal is to tell the story of someone who has recovered from a health scare, bereavement or disappointment and who can show readers how it is possible to overcome these difficulties. You can either interview them or re-tell their story if it is not your own.

You are unlikely to be able to do this anonymously, as the editor will want a photo, so make sure everyone involved is happy for the details to become public.

Some examples of stories that have been published recently include success with internet dating, surviving a double mastectomy, helping someone with postnatal depression and beating alcoholism.

Tips and hints

There must be so many tips and techniques you could write about, including those on health, fitness, beauty, gardening, photography or car maintenance that it should be easy to write up one in detail or collect together a few on the same topic and present them as a filler. If you have tried and failed to get an article published that was in this form, split up your tips and present them as fillers to different magazines. Some examples I have found recently include: "3 steps to a better lawn", "top 10 foods that heal", "5 ways to recycle old tights" and "what shoppers need to know – a roundup of consumer law".

EXAMPLE
After publishing a book on finding work when you're over 50, My Weekly asked me to write a piece offering some job hunting tips. I picked five: your application, the perfect CV, the interview, awkward questions and final decisions.

Humour

The best advice for this area is to keep your eyes and ears open. Any day of the week you can overhear funny conversations, see people doing daft things, discover strange entries in newspapers or magazines or have a "senior moment" that made you laugh. A photograph is wonderful but just a recounted joke may get you a small payment.

Latest news

This type of filler is normally prepared by staff writers or the editor, especially as they receive samples and publicity material all the time, but if you are in the business or have some extra knowledge of relevant products or activities, you may be able to carve a niche for yourself in this area.

Special events

Did you know that there is a Sweeps Festival the first weekend of May, and National Doodle Day is 2nd March?

If you want to write about national days of any kind and live in the UK, a good place to start is www.projectbritain.com/calendars. This site provides a list of hundreds of events celebrated in Britain. It includes holidays, awareness days, festivals and unusual customs and traditions and if there is one, it offers a link to a relevant website where you will find more information.

As most magazines will cover the well-known days like Halloween, Easter Day and Bonfire Night, try to find a more obscure event to write about.

When you sit down to write your filler, one approach is to start with the day itself, e.g. Apple Day (October 21st) and then identify a suitable gardening, cooking, supermarket or health publication to slant it towards. You would probably want to start by introducing the special day and then offer the appropriate information or advice as the main content of your filler.

EXAMPLE
Cookery magazine slants for Apple Day might include:
- *an apple pie/cake/pudding or savoury recipe*
- *advice on storing apples*
- *the difference between eating and cooking apples when baking*
- *which apple varieties are best in the kitchen?*

Gardening magazine slants might include:
- *Growing an apple tree*
- *Gardens to visit that have Apple Day activities*
- *Pruning an apple tree*
- *Apple varieties to grow, or that are dying out*

Alternatively, choose a magazine or journal category and then find out if there are any relevant days to research. For example, if you'd like to write for a cookery or food magazine, relevant days or events might be cheese rolling, apples, chips, pancakes (Shrove Tuesday), Fair Trade goods, food safety, farmhouse breakfast and British Food Fortnight. (National Doodle Day, of course, would be very appropriate for a painting magazine.)

Either way, it is important to remember that publications take several months to prepare for print (although this may be less true for web-based pages), and so you must pitch or send in your item months before the date.

EXERCISE 41
1. *Use the Project Britain website or a similar one and locate a national day that is quite new to you but that you feel would*

be of interest to magazine readers. Make sure it is at least six months away.

2. *Find a suitable magazine to write for.*

3. *Write a short filler, keeping it light-hearted but factual. If you have a personal anecdote that relates to it and, definitely, if you can take some photos, that would be especially valuable.*

4. *Send off your piece in good time.*

REVIEWS

There are several approaches you can take when writing reviews:

1. Review one item in depth
2. Compare two similar items
3. Collect together several items under a common theme

SINGLE REVIEWS

If you really want to review restaurants, TV or radio programmes, films, books or entertainment events such as music gigs or festivals, target small publishers both on and offline, lesser known journals or regionally distributed magazines or newspapers and you will have a far better chance of getting your reviews accepted than if you try to compete nationally.

When reviewing, it is very important to bear the reader in mind, and so your language and writing style must fit the publications you approach. It is important to write a truthful and honest review based on your own experience (not second-hand material you have read elsewhere) and to provide all the necessary and relevant details that anyone deciding to follow up a review and buy the product or visit the place for themselves would need to have. For example, it may require contact details, product name, price, manufacturer, size, ambience or supplier, depending on what you are reviewing.

Most important, any positive or negative statements of opinion should be restrained rather than extreme or over-the-top, and based on reasoned and convincing evidence. If you are allergic to tuna and chose to eat a tuna sandwich, for example, it is only fair to explain why you were ill after a visit, rather than condemn the sandwich bar out of hand.

Book reviews

Look widely for markets as there are websites constantly springing up such as www.thebookbag.co.uk or www.bookgeeks.co.uk that welcome readers' book reviews and may provide free books as some form of payment. Remember that getting reviews published online with a reputable website without payment can be the start of a credible portfolio to present to a paying publication. Many national papers also print a few readers' book reviews now and again on a themed page.

EXAMPLE
Reviews are often rejected because they don't do a good enough job. Here is some sound advice from Antony Jones who runs www.sfbooks.com: "The review should describe, analyze, evaluate and above all entertain, conveying your own opinion with supporting evidence from the book itself. Don't forget that this is your own personal view so don't be afraid of saying how you feel or what you really thought."

If you have any specialist knowledge, the area of technical and scientific journals may be worth pursuing e.g. the Journal of Clinical Nursing publishes advice about reviewing for them at www.blackwellpublishing.com/pdf/jcn_reviewers.pdf and this advice is likely to be helpful for other specialists to follow. There are also entire journals devoted to book reviews such as The London Review of Books that would normally expect you to have a suitable academic or professional background but will look at any review you submit.

EXERCISE 42
1. *Go to http://www.bookgeeks.co.uk/become-a-bookgeek/ or http://www.thebookbag.co.uk/reviews/index.php?title=Reviewer_Vacancies and read the guidelines.*
2. *Write and submit a book review.*

Products and services

As well as books, you can review anything from goods to services, so an experience with a retailer, tea shop, training course, pizza delivery, new car, kitchen appliance, travel agent, stove installer, nursery or government department may be worth something to a suitable publisher. One choice to make is whether you want to name the product, service provider or company or if you prefer to draw general conclusions from your encounter.

COMPARISONS

A common approach with reviews is to compare a number of similar items or services, rather than review just one in depth. This is a common format in women's and cookery magazines as they often carry reviews of three or four different moisturisers, lipsticks, sauces, packets of biscuits or jams.

EXAMPLE

Having taken two very different distance learning writing courses, I wrote an in-depth comparison for Writers' Forum which was published with the title "Find one that fits".

Scope is the online journal of film and TV studies produced by Nottingham University and the publishers say:" we are particularly keen to publish book-review essays of 2,000-3,500 words. We presently do not seek reviews of single books, but ask that prospective reviewers choose two or more titles that could be included in an omnibus review. A list of books currently available for review is posted on the website."

EXERCISE 43

1. *Tour your town or village or think about your local area and identify three or four similar establishments that are special to the place such as potteries, wine cellars or children's entertainment centres, or that are provided particularly for tourists or holidaymakers such as tea rooms, boats for hire or gift shops.*

2. *Plan out a review that compares the pros and cons of the various enterprises.*

3. *Find a local paper or regional magazine that might be interested in your article and send them a query letter.*

****

CH. 8

WRITING BOOKS

If you have been working through this guide and carried out the exercises in earlier chapters you will have developed some good ideas for topics you could write about in articles and features. Very often, these will have been based on one-off experiences, encounters or events.

Although your ideas may well be an excellent starting point, a book needs quite a large volume of data and so you are going to have to select subjects that are appropriate for book form and can either be based on these earlier ideas expanded to fill several hundred pages, or that are completely new topics. Just like a short story often doesn't translate well into a film because it feels too "thin", so it may be necessary to start again when planning to write an entire book.

EXERCISE 44
1. *Look through your own book shelves or visit a bookshop or the library and wander through the non-fiction isles.*
2. *Make a note of any interesting or amusing titles.*
3. *How many different types of book can you find?*

Here are ten random books I found when I carried out this activity recently:

- Things Get Better – a personal account of life after a trauma by Katie Piper, who suffered an acid attack
- Narrow Boat – an exploration of the British canal system written in 1944
- You Can Paint – a 'how to' guide to watercolour painting for beginners
- Client Centred Therapy - an in-depth look at a counselling methodology

- Go It Alone – advice on becoming self-employed
- Professor Stewart's Cabinet of Mathematical Curiosities – a collection of mathematical puzzles and stories
- London's Old Buildings – an exploration of London architecture
- Linda Goodman's Sun Signs – the astrology of every sign of the Zodiac
- The Nation's Favourite Shakespeare – a collection of extracts from plays and sonnets
- Complete Letter Writer – specimen letters for all occasions

There are many different types of non-fiction book that you could write. Some of the most common categories include:

1. Self-help or how to books that encourage readers to achieve a goal by setting out all the steps they can take e.g. to run a business, train for a marathon, overcome drugs, be happy or keep chickens

2. Reference books such as atlases, dictionaries or classifications of items such as butterflies or wine – either produced as volumes of lasting value or books that will need to be updated annually

3. Textbooks and course books

4. A collection of interviews, profiles, letters, travelogues or articles on a set theme that make use of previous writings

5. A tract to persuade readers of a viewpoint where background, historical data, quotations, statistics, case studies etc. are all needed to make the case

6. An in-depth exploration or comprehensive coverage of one subject, for example: a country, a political system, a work of literature, a solar system, one animal species, an abstract idea like advertising or the life of one person (biography)

7. Autobiography or memoirs left for posterity or to provide an insight into personal experience e.g. of being an actor, starting a business or living abroad

8. Entertainment books such as joke books
9. Another book in an established series, if you can spot a gap
10. A recognisable type of book such as a travel guide, cookery book, diet book or children's activity book
11. A vehicle for promoting photographs or art work

WHY YOUR BOOK IS WORTH WRITING

Like most things in life, it is hard to be completely original as a writer and there is often more than one book on the topic of your choice that has already been published. But even if this is the case, there are many reasons why yours could still be worth writing and publishing.

FILL A GAP IN THE MARKET

It is quite common to search for but fail to find a book on a topic of interest, or believe that a group or situation is not being catered for and the idea for a new book may suddenly spring to mind. If you are lucky enough to have a good idea for a book and find nothing is available that covers your subject, the obvious answer is to write it yourself.

In some cases, your idea for filling a gap may fit in well with a current series or specialised publisher and so it may be easy to convince them that this book is needed. For example, when the "For Dummies" series first started, it concentrated on computing and you may well have been an expert on one particular software package that had not yet been covered. Nowadays, they seem to cover ever topic imaginable and so you would find it much harder to get your idea accepted. In the same way, the publishers Search Press are well-known for their craft books and if you were knowledgeable about enamelling you would see that they have only published one book on this subject (in 2004) and it is likely that there would be lots of room for another one.

In most cases, you are going to have to persuade the publishers that the gap in the market not only exists but that they would gain by being the first to publish a book on the subject.

EXAMPLE

When I was an IT lecturer I needed a computing book with enough exercises to keep my class working for 30 – 40 minutes, but after looking on the shelves of various bookshops I could only find "How to" books. Very few contained more than just one or two exercises to accompany each topic. After writing a large number of exercises for my own teaching, these were eventually published by Pearsons as "Practical Exercises for ECDL". The publisher could see that such exercises would be a resource that would appeal to other lecturers by saving them time writing their own material and added an extra selling point– a link to a well-known vocational qualification.

Sadly, if you are the first to market with a particular book you will have to be prepared to be copied. Good book ideas are often mimicked as there is no copyright on ideas or even book titles, and you are quite likely to be followed by others hanging onto your coat tails. My book, for example, was followed a few years' later by someone else writing "ECDL Practice Exercises", and not only was the format very similar, they even copied my idea of including some exercises in the form of a crossword.

WRITE A BETTER BOOK

Who hasn't finished reading a book and decided that it was either so bad that it should never have been published, or it would have benefited from a completely different approach? Perhaps it needed case studies, exercises, examples or interviews; a chapter offering further resources; less waffle or personal anecdotes and more factual information; cartoons and jokes; or whole sections added or removed.

As long as you write a much better book, it may not take long before yours becomes the accepted publication in its field.

CHANGE THE EMPHASIS

Even if other books on the same topic are very successful, yours will be different by default, as you are a different person and will have a different writing style and approach to the subject. There is normally room in the market for more than one book covering the same topic as long as yours is distinctive and you can offer a Unique Selling Point (USP). Then, you should still be able to make your book a success. Perhaps yours will be more up-to-date; aimed at a different age group; easier to read; better structured; better illustrated; will have accompanying discs or website material; or your subject will be treated more imaginatively e.g. seen from a fantasy character's point of view. Whatever you put into your own book, if it is different for a good reason it can still see off rivals - even those that are already well established.

EXAMPLE

According to Amazon, there are over 800 books available at the moment offering advice on giving wedding speeches. Even the same publisher, How To Books, has thought it worth including several books on the subject in its lists. They have published the following books by different authors: "Making the Father of the Bride's Speech", "How to Make A Great Wedding Speech", "Wedding Speeches for Women", "Raise Your Glasses, Please" and "Be the Best, Best Man and Make a Stunning Speech".

As well as these five publications, they also publish: "Wedding Speeches and Etiquette", "Father of the Bride: Speech and Duties", "Making the Bridegroom's Speech", "The Complete Best Man", "Making the Best Man's Speech" and "Making a Wedding Speech" by the same author as that of the first book.

Sometimes you may be able to find a publisher that has "missed the boat" or not been bold enough to dip their toe into that particular water even though they would be expected to have kept up with their rivals in the same field. Here, you may be able to fill a gap in "their" provision, rather than in the book world as a whole, but that is still a perfectly valid reason for your book to be published.

EXERCISE 45

1. *Take any topic you might write about e.g. Volcanoes and see how many books you can find on Amazon or library catalogue searches that cover the same topic.*

2. *Now see how many of these take your preferred approach such as "inside a volcano", a children's book on volcanoes or volcanoes of the Mediterranean and decide if your book would fill a gap or if it would need to be a different or better book than those already available.*

3. *If there are one or more books covering your topic already, look through their contents list and any sample chapters to see if you can spot anything that your book would do better, or that is missing altogether. If not, how could you make your own book stand out?*

FINDING THE SUBJECT

As well as getting ideas for books from the current, inadequate provision or after searching for a book that you need but that has not yet been written, ideas also come from overheard conversations, inventions and discoveries, TV or radio programmes or other people's suggestions. Many subjects come from writers' own backgrounds and Chapter 2 offered a range of techniques for identifying personal interests, experiences or skills that you could write about.

When I look at the books I have published, I find I have written about:

- Computing aimed at the general public (building on my work as an IT tutor)
- Computing as course books (requested by a publisher to fill a gap in general provision)
- Digital cameras (an idea that came from the publishers to compliment their computing books and fill a gap in their provision)
- Finding work (based on my work as a Careers Adviser)

- Cooking garden produce (from an interest in cooking and gardening, sparked off by trying to solve a problem of too many runner beans)
- Writing an autobiography (this came about after a distance learning college where I worked first suggested this as a coursework publication and I then expanded it into a book)

As you can see from my personal list, not all are based on work experience or personal interest. Some resulted from suggestions from publishers themselves. Being commissioned to write a book often happens once you have written a few successful books, and as long as you have a good relationship with your editors.

OPINIONS AND BELIEFS

Many books are written from a desire to communicate ideas, beliefs or views on subjects that authors feel strongly about. Perhaps you want to:

Make science more fun for children

Help people understand ethics

Encourage a way of life such as downsizing or bartering

Warn people of the dangers of caffeine

Put the record straight on dieting, anorexia or employment law

Persuade people to drink more English wine

Whatever your purpose, all that is needed is to research the topic thoroughly, organise the material so that your message is clear, and write in the most informative and entertaining manner possible.

EXERCISE 46

1. *Do you have any burning issues you want to communicate, or any long-term ambitions to write a particular book?*
2. *Have you spotted any gaps in the market or any books you could write better?*
3. *Have you identified any topics from your own background that would make a good book?*

4. *For each of these ideas, what is the best treatment?*

5. *Make a list of 5 – 10 books you might write and put them in order of priority e.g. starting with the easiest, the most enjoyable or where you think there is the most need.*

AUTOBIOGRAPHY

If you want to write about your own life, there are a number of relevant books on the market offering guidance. In particular, they will show you:

- how to remember your past
- how to identify and put forward your main message
- how to decide what to include and what to leave out
- how to order and organise your material
- what formats you could use for your final publication
- how to deal with the thorny issues of privacy, hurting people's feelings or family secrets

A key problem will be publication. Unless you are a celebrity, or have fascinating connections, world-shattering experiences or unusual skeletons in the cupboard, you may not find any publisher interested in bringing out a book on your life. That is because they won't believe there is a wide enough audience for it.

This may be a case for self-publishing, which is covered in a later section.

THE CONTENTS

Once you have your topic and some idea of how it is going to be treated, you need to get down to the details.

TITLES

In Chapter 6 I provided a list of sources of ideas for titles that you might find helpful. You could also look through books in the same genre or on the same topic and see what other authors have called their own books, to give you more ideas.

EXERCISE 47

1. *Imagine you have decided to write a book on the history of paper and want to write a straightforward, informative book aimed at the general public.*
2. *Think up at least five different titles for your book that you believe will make people want to read it.*
3. *Test them out on family and friends to see which works best and why.*

ORGANISING YOUR BOOK

There are a number of ways to organise the contents of a book, and even if you have written several books already it is still hard to make those final decisions for any new body of work. Fortunately, one of the best approaches is to start with other people's books.

Whether or not you are going to cover subject matter that has already been written about, you should be able to gather together several books in the public domain that are of the same genre or aimed at the same audience. (Make sure they are well written and that they have received reasonable reviews on websites such as Amazon as you only want to learn from the best.)

You don't need to buy any copies unless you actually want to own them. Many will be available from your local library but if not, search for them at Google books (http://books.google.co.uk/books), download a free ebook sample or see if they offer an Amazon "Click to Look Inside" facility at http://www.amazon.co.uk.

Read any books you get hold of all the way through and for the others, most books now have an online presence and you should find at least a contents list and samples from some of the chapters. If you only have the book online, don't forget to check the index at the back as well as the main contents - there is often a great deal of extra information here about what is included.

As you work through these various publications, take notes on how you are feeling about both content and structure and ask yourself lots of questions, such as:

Do the topics follow naturally?

Are there useful sections you wouldn't have thought of including?

Are there any gaps?

If included, how many exercises, case studies, quotations etc are there?

Are these in the right places and are there too many or not enough?

How well is the book illustrated?

You should find that by the third book you sample, you are getting a good idea of how you would want to organise your own book, what you now want to include and what doesn't seem to work. In other words, you will be finding your voice in terms of the structure of the book you want to write.

I should add that reading other people's books is also a good way to discover that you strongly dislike the idea of doing what has been done before. If you come up with a completely original approach, as long as you are sure your structure will work and will provide a palatable experience for readers, so much the better.

EXERCISE 48

Before you start this exercise, note down your preferred contents list if you have already spent time planning a book. This may still turn out to be the best design, but you can test it out at Step 4.

1. *Take your own or any topic you might possibly write about e.g. "Tortoises", identify the genre or type of book e.g. "How to look after...." and search for one or more books already published on this topic that are either in the library or at least offer a view of the main contents on the Web. If there are no books exactly the same, try to find something as similar as you can that would be aimed at the same audience e.g. How to look after your snake/gerbil/parrot. Don't forget to vary your search key words or check out various book series. Examples of phrases to look for would include: Keeping a....Living with*

*a ...... Training a....Pet Owners Guide to... Caring for a...
or Tortoises/Snakes/Gerbils for Dummies ...etc.*

2. *Work through the contents list and index of each book and read as many sample chapters as you can, thinking about the structure.*

3. *If you can get hold of copies, read the books all the way through and ask yourself lots of questions as you do so.*

4. *Now spend some time planning out your own contents list or working on your original ideas for a book. Add, reorganise or cut material so that you end up with a plan you are comfortable with. It is likely to be quite different from and far superior to the structure of the books you have been analysing.*

5. *If you are ready, start breaking down the chapters so that you can describe exactly what each one might cover. (Once you get to this stage - all that is left is to write the book!!!)*

APPENDICES AND ILLUSTRATIONS

Any material that doesn't really fit easily and logically within a book itself is normally added as one or more appendices. Depending on the type of book you are writing, there may be supplementary material or extra features that you want to include. If these may not be relevant to all readers, you can make them available at the back of the book where they can be referred to by those who are particularly interested but will not annoy readers who don't want to look at them. Examples include maps, facsimiles of documents, coloured photographs, sheet music, family trees, recommended reading, glossaries, or sample letters and quotations.

EXAMPLE
A book aimed at friends of those bereaved called "If there's anything I can do..." by Caroline Doughty has two appendices: a list of things not to say to someone who has been widowed and advice on identifying signs of depression.

When I wrote an Age Concern book of computing activities for elderly computer users, it followed on from an introductory book and so I didn't want to repeat all the general instructions about using a computer. The publishers felt that some readers might not be as competent as others (or wouldn't have read the earlier book) and so an appendix was added containing a summarised version of the basic skills needed.

Illustrations can either be added at the end in an appendix or can be dotted throughout the book. Sometimes they are collected together in batches after every two or three chapters. Small drawings, screen prints, diagrams, graphs or photographs of food items are usually placed within the relevant chapters as they are usually being described or referred to in the text. However, if there are large colour plates or photos of locations or family portraits in a biography or history book, they may be fine displayed together somewhere apart from within the main body of the text, as long as they are well captioned. Even if you have a strong view about how and where you want illustrations, the book designer is likely to have the last word as publishers usually like their books to look similar or to keep to a standard design brief. There is also the matter of colours and sizes and the relationship of these to printing costs.

PERMISSIONS

Your own photos, drawings and paintings will be copyright free, but to use anyone else's work can be tricky. If it cannot be avoided, you or staff in the publishing house may spend a great deal of time trying to contact companies, artists, websites and photographic agencies to get permission to use material or to negotiate the cost of doing so. Don't forget that quotations from books, poems and songs are also copyright protected.

FORMATS

Most authors have little or no say in the size of their book, the cover picture, the colours or tones of ink, the formatting of fonts for headings and sub-headings, whether it is hard or paperback, the price, the navigational clues, the spine binding, the way pictures are presented, or much else. You may be consulted on some of these, of course, but do not expect to be able to over-ride your editor.

If there are some books on a similar theme that you really like the look of, your best hope is to make a successful submission to one of the publishers concerned as you are then more likely to be happy with the look of your finished book.

FINDING A PUBLISHER

If you want your book published by a mainstream publisher and you have worked on your book and have a good idea of where it is going in terms of subject matter, content and style, it is time to find a named publisher to approach. For non-fiction, you do not have to have completed the book before making contact and you certainly don't need to waste money on a literary agent acting on your behalf (see below for more on agents).

Up until a few years ago, writers were always directed to two reference books: The Writers & Artists Yearbook and The Writers' Handbook, which contain lists of agents, publishers, editors and the like. However, I believe that the Internet has made these largely redundant. This is because it is now so easy to carry out a search for publishers, even the most obscure and little-known ones, that relying on a printed book that takes at least a year to compile simply cannot make sense.

To find a possible publisher:

- Carry out a book search in library or bookshop catalogues to see how many books have already been written on a *similar* subject. For example, if you want to write about caring for tortoises, why not search for "rabbit" or "pet" non-fiction books? Once you find a few you like the look of, you can note down the names of the publishers.

- Now, carry out a second search, but this time look through those particular publishers' book lists, to check that they haven't already published one on tortoises.
- Carry out this type of publisher search as well if you already have a named publisher in mind (perhaps recommended to you) and don't want to submit a proposal for a book they have already published.

Even if you identify a few publishers in the right field who currently have not produced any "tortoise" books, they may have one in the pipeline. To check this out, you could look for a list of "forthcoming books" on their website. If there is no mention of tortoises, there is a good chance that they will be open to your ideas.

SUBMISSION DOCUMENTS

With fiction, it is quite impossible to get the true flavour of a book, play or film from a summary of its plot. For example, the story of a boy falling in love with his friend's mother but they eventually decide to part could be written as a romance, horror story, tragedy, comedy, science fiction or thriller. For non-fiction, editors won't normally need to read an entire book to understand its scope and purpose. Instead, you are expected to send them enough information to allow them to decide if your project is worth taking on.

Most will publish submission guidelines on their websites or can send you a copy setting out exactly what they want to learn about you and your proposed book. Often, it will also state the types of book that don't interest them.

Take note from one firm who speak for all when they say: "As you will appreciate, only a small proportion of the manuscripts submitted to publishers are finally accepted for publication. Some of these are not looked at because the publisher's particular submission procedure was not adhered to or was ignored."

LITERARY AGENTS

Literary agents are people who have set themselves up to act as the middle (wo)men between authors and publishers. As so many unknown writers want to write fiction, and fiction has to be read before you know whether it is saleable or not, agents are paid to weed out much of the unprintable and then pass on suggested books to publishing houses they have good contacts with and whose needs they understand. For this job, they tend to be paid something like 15% of the income the author will earn. They also act on behalf of authors when it comes to contracts, rights and other technical or legal aspects of publishing.

In the world of non-fiction, an agent is usually unnecessary. If you send a list of chapters and an overall summary of a textbook, biography, popular science, self-help or recipe book to an appropriate publisher, it won't take them very long to understand the concept and they can then ask for further information and sample chapters if they like the idea and think it might be worth pursuing.

There are some agents who do work with non-fiction authors and if you feel strongly that you would like to use one (and this may be necessary if you are writing an autobiography or travel book that errs towards creative non-fiction and where the writing style and approach may be more important than its contents), you can find lists of agencies to contact in reference books or by searching online.

WHAT EDITORS WANT TO KNOW

Just as query letters are needed to sell article ideas, so book editors will want to know:

- What the book is about
- What type of book you are writing e.g. a biography, "how to" or textbook etc.
- The approach you are taking e.g. a personal view, interviews with practitioners or self-help advice

- The exact contents and any extra features such as exercises, case studies or sample question papers
- Why this book is needed now
- The market for this book – both the main audience and secondary readers
- What is its main competition (by name, if possible) and how yours differs (i.e. its Unique Selling Points)
- If you can help sell the book (personal contacts etc)
- How it fits in with their current list and preferred genres
- Why you are the right person to write this book (i.e. your credentials)
- That you can write
- You will deliver on time and at the required standard

On a separate note, just as a story can play an important role in a non-fiction feature or book chapter, so a personal story of why or how you came to write your book may persuade an otherwise sceptical editor to take it on, so do include it as long as it is part of the overall submission and is kept short and to the point.

SYNOPSIS

A book proposal is a little like a book review, although a proposal should definitely not include personal opinions (such as "what a brilliant book this is!"). Perhaps a well-written proposal is more like the covering letter that goes with a CV, "selling" the applicant (but without any hard sell as such) and ensuring that they are selected for the next stage of the process.

In some writing guides and websites, the term "synopsis" is used to describe the entire proposal, but as there are so many parts of a proposal you need to write, I am defining synopsis in a narrower sense, as a general summary by which you can tell editors succinctly what your book is about and how you are approaching the subject. What is needed is a short description of the book content in general (but not setting out every chapter) and its overall aim. Somewhere, include a mention of one or two of the best or unique features.

If you think up a really good title for you book (see earlier for some ideas), this can help in the sales pitch.

EXERCISE 49

1. *Take any non-fiction book that you have enjoyed reading (or your own book if it has progressed far enough) and write a 250 - 500 word synopsis that explains what the book is about and the approach you or the author has taken.*

2. *Without using any hard-sell, write it so that it would encourage people to want to read it and make sure it mentions any special features.*

3. *Try to think up your own alternative title for the book.*

Book contents

Somewhere in your submission you need to send a full chapter list for the book so that editors know exactly what you propose to cover. For each chapter, unless it is self-evident, write a short summary or include sub-headings so that the content is clear.

Perhaps at the end of the list, mention any extra features you are hoping to include such as a compact disk of files or photos; sample exam papers with answers; sample form letters; interviews; graphs or illustrations; case studies or a glossary.

Why this particular book

You will need to convince an editor that your book is needed and that it will sell. This is particularly important if it is not the type of book they usually publish (although they are still a sensible choice for it), or if it is slightly risky.

This is the place to set out your reasons for coming up with the idea, such as:

- Identifying an obvious gap in the market that you can describe clearly, perhaps the topic has not been covered or you have identified a group of readers that are not being catered for
- Linking it to a particular trend or current topic of interest where there is a ready audience
- Feeling it would complete a particular series or set of books that they already publish
- Being uniquely qualified to write this particular book, perhaps to share best practice or because there are no publications as expert as yours will be

The market

Some books have a ready market and these are the easiest to sell to a publisher. These include textbooks or course books that cover a current syllabus: school, college or university students obviously need up-to-date books to help them through their courses. In other cases, you will need to do some research to find out who might be interested in buying your book and what that means in terms of numbers of potential readers/purchasers. For example, is there a clear and growing interest in the topic? If so, try to find evidence in the form of social trends that you can quote or figures available on government websites that show an undeniable growth in certain practices, groups of people, leisure pursuits or work activities.

Let's say that you have statistical evidence or can point to changes in the law that show more people are living longer; children must now learn foreign languages in primary school; or young couples have to rent rather than buy their homes. This will make it far easier to persuade an editor that a book on *Life after 80*, *French for five-year-olds* or *Renting in the 21st Century* will sell.

Even if nothing has changed that you can pinpoint, you still need to identify your audience clearly. So if you have plans for a cookery book, tell the editor if your book is specifically:

- For the disabled
- Aimed at carers looking after the elderly in their own homes
- Relevant to dads bringing up their kids alone
- A teenager's first cookery book, or
- For fast food eaters who want a healthier version of their favourite snacks

Explain why it is needed and how you aim to cater for your chosen readership.

When setting out who the book is aimed at, you may need to mention both your primary target (the main readers you have in mind) and the secondary target (people who could benefit from or enjoy your book as well.)

For example, if you were writing a book of computing activities specifically aimed at teachers for use in the classroom (the primary target), your secondary audience could be parents and grandparents who could supervise the activities at home, or even older children who might carry them out on their own. Again, a book on astronomy might be aimed primarily at people who have bought their first home telescope, but the secondary target could be science teachers or FE tutors running astronomy classes or clubs in schools and colleges.

EXERCISE 50
1. *Take a topic you hope to write about, or select one from potential article material that you have already identified or written about.*
2. *Why would a book on this subject be needed?*
3. *Who should it primarily be aimed at?*
4. *Who else might buy this book?*

Competition

You should always do some research into the books that are out there, to check the viability of any of your own book ideas: would yours be the first or 50th book on this topic? For a proposal, you need to note down the actual titles and publishers of books that seem closest to your own, as well as the overall numbers of books in that category.

If yours would be the first, you don't have too much of a problem with competition. It is far more likely that you can identify 10 – 20 books that would be classed as similar and perhaps 5 – 10 that have chosen to treat the subject in the same way. Here, it is important to read and find out as much as you can about these books (by looking at actual library or bookshop copies or reading online extracts and checking out any book reviews) so that you can say in your submission how you can compete successfully with any other publications currently available.

EXAMPLE

Checking on Amazon for rivals to my proposed book on "Making the Most of your Glorious Glut", I discovered that there were only 10 other books with the word "glut" in the title, and most of these were in German. Broadening the search, I found another 22 books providing advice for people with allotments and so I had to look closely at all these. I discovered that there wasn't a direct rival but of those that were similar, many:

- *only covered a single or limited number of vegetables or fruits*
- *were very out-of-date*
- *concentrated on growing rather than storing and cooking*
- *contained too much advice on storage at the expense of enough recipes*
- *were very badly and unattractively produced*
- *didn't limit themselves to food types that we grow too much of in the UK*
- *were quite expensive, so out of the reach of most people*
- *were organised alphabetically by named fruit or vegetable and so duplicated many of the categories (e.g. a recipe for gooseberry jam under G, raspberry jam under R, blackcurrant jam under B, strawberry jam under S etc)*

From this, I was able to say that my book would be unique because it:

- *covered only UK produce that we tend to grow too much of*
- *would concentrate on processes (such as jam-making, drying or bottling) to prevent duplication of recipes and make the most flexible use of different fruit or vegetables, and*
- *would include both advice on all types of storing, drying, preserving, bottling and freezing as well as over 250 recipes.*

I would also be able to make the case for an attractively produced book containing good quality photos that should be priced under £15.

EXERCISE 51

1. *Try to identify a specific topic you might write a book about.*
2. *Carry out a careful search for similar books aimed at your selected primary target.*
3. *Identify the one that seems to offer the stiffest competition i.e. the one that has chosen the same treatment and looks attractive and well written.*
4. *How could you compete with this book, if a publisher was interested in publishing yours? In other words, what is (are) your Unique Selling Point(s)?*

Why this particular publisher

To be honest, most authors are delighted if anyone wants to publish their book, but there is usually a hierarchy of mainstream publishers you are most drawn to.

To convince a publisher that they have been chosen, you need to have some good reasons. For example:

- They publish very similar books and yours would fit in well
- They produce a series and yours would fill a gap

- They have a good reputation for this type of book (e.g. textbooks, biographies, green issues, self help, humorous books etc)
- You have seen on their website that they particularly welcome new authors
- They are seeking more books in the category you are writing about

(You may not want to mention this, but you might also choose a publisher because they are not limiting submissions to those coming through an agent.)

Credentials

A background in your area of expertise and/or writing and publishing experience are usually essential, especially to publishers who may be taking quite a risk with an author who is unknown or they have not published before. So it is very important when trying to find a publisher to tell them as much as you can about your relevant background and experience.

In some cases, if your idea is good enough, you may be able to persuade them by emphasising the point of the book, rather than relying on your background or qualifications. Here, you will need to work particularly hard to convince them that you can also write and deliver on time.

If sending a CV, don't forget to rewrite it for the world of publishing if it is one you have been using for other things. List all publications or work related to editing/language/communicating etc as well as your specialist knowledge or connection to the specific topic or style of book you want to write.

EXERCISE 52
1. *Take a topic for a book you are thinking of writing or have started to write.*

2. *Note down all the experience, qualifications and knowledge you have of this topic, citing actual evidence where possible.*
3. *Note down any relevant experience or abilities you have in the field of writing.*
4. *Note down any evidence that you complete tasks, can manage projects or anything else that might be relevant.*
5. *Now draft out a convincing statement why you are the right person to write this book.*

Nowadays, marketing books is a difficult, expensive and cut-throat business and many publishers are looking for help from authors themselves. If you are known locally, carry out activities where you will meet hundreds of potential purchasers or can get publicity for your book through radio or TV programmes or in the local paper, the publishers are more likely to be interested as the book will sell more effectively.

EXAMPLE

Pegasus Elliot Mackenzie Publishers offer this advice to novice authors:
"Many authors may already have an independent but non-writing career which has ensured previous public acclaim for related good works, charity fund raising, local voluntary work in the community, etc. This can mean that they would be already acknowledged by their local media, e.g. in newspaper articles, or have acquired for themselves a degree of fame. This is an important asset and should be mentioned when submitting work for publication."

Can you write?

You will need to send one or two complete chapters. These will show the editor not only that you can write but also that you are able to sustain a consistent style and tone throughout the book and that it reads well. Even if you are a "good" writer, you may have an academic, over-flowery or stiff style that doesn't sit well with your subject matter or proposed audience, and it is important for them to discover this before you exchange contracts.

In many cases, the introduction or first chapter is written quite late by authors. Unless the publishers specify particular chapters in their submission guidelines, it should be fine to send them any examples of completed chapters that you are happy with or even excerpts from several, to display your writing skills and approach to best effect.

Can you deliver?

In most cases, publishing is not an instant business and you would normally have up to a year to produce a finished manuscript. Even if you don't think you'll need it, it is worth trying to negotiate a reasonably lengthy timescale so that you make sure you can meet any final and important deadlines.

Chapter 10 offers advice if you suddenly develop writer's block or don't feel you can finish the work, but it tends to seem much harder at the beginning and once you start writing it may well flow easily.

I find writing the very beginning of some books the hardest and often start in the middle with material I am most confident about; there are no rules about how to write as long as you get started and keep going.

THE NEXT STEP

If your submission is accepted, the editor will get in touch and you can move on to the next step. This will be to discuss the timing, organisation and approach (if the publisher has different ideas to yours), before the issuing of a contract (see the next section).

Your book may be partly or even completely written, but there may well be extensive rewriting required and any extra features that are needed will have to be added. You will also need to source and then check if any photographs, screen prints from the Web, quotations or other inclusions require permission from the authors (because of copyright) and may be asked to follow these up yourself. The word count will be agreed in advance and so you may also have to spend time adding or cutting material to end up with the correct length of manuscript.

Eventually, you will be sending off copies of the first draft in print and/or on CD or by email and these will be returned to you as proofs. As well as checking these yourself, the publishing firm will have its own proof readers who check manuscripts carefully for grammar, punctuation and spelling errors and all the other things that can go wrong such as the omission or transposition of blocks of text or whole chapters; inadequate case studies or answers to questions; incorrect or inconsistent weights and measures; or hanging references (where you refer readers to another section that doesn't exist).

Sadly, there is not that much professional checking going on. If you are not writing an opinion piece and are not completely on top of your subject, it is easy to make serious professional errors such as not covering a full syllabus, getting scientific, historical or technical facts wrong or providing the wrong answers to questions. These may only be picked up after the first editions are printed. It is very expensive (and embarrassing) to recall and reprint books, so you might like to draw on the kindness of colleagues or other contacts to check your work beforehand, if you feel that it might be possible to make errors.

PUBLICITY

Well before a book comes out, the marketing department will be trying to promote it. This is often the main reason for choosing to publish with a mainstream publisher and so you will need to help as much as you can. This may involve:

- Providing lists of contacts (ideally in the media or well-known figures) who can be approached for quotes, reviews or publicity
- Writing a short biography as well as a "blurb" about the book to go in press releases or on the book cover
- Providing photographs
- Being available for interviews – in print or TV and radio
- Writing short pieces about the book that can be sent out to magazines and journals or used for flyers

- Being available for signings or even interviews, festivals and workshops when the book comes out
- Being active locally to help promote your book to bookshops or newspapers

EXERCISE 53

1. *Imagine your book has been accepted and is going to be published by a large publishing house.*
2. *List as many relevant contacts you have and any ideas for promoting your book.*

CONTRACTS

The Publishers Association produces a code of practice which sets out what contracts should contain and how publishers should treat their authors. When you receive your contract and start working with a publisher, you should make sure that:

- The wording is clear and unambiguous, including any option clauses or in relation to royalties or updating. It should be honoured in both the spirit and letter
- It is clear about the ownership of the copyright now and in the future
- They honour your moral rights (for example, if they want to include material you object to)
- They offer you the chance to share in the success of your work
- They handle matters promptly and keep you fully informed
- They do not cancel the contract without good reason
- Changes are specified clearly and are reasonable
- If they decide to reject the work, they treat you fairly and have a proper complaints procedure
- The timescale is reasonable and clear
- They support you if, through no fault of your own, you breach any rules e.g. on copyright or data protection

- They help with extra costs that may need to be incurred
- You receive regular information about your earnings and are paid promptly and in full
- They discuss design or marketing issues or decisions with you
- You are offered remaindered stock
- The relationship is one of cooperation

On your side, you must be honest about the ownership of the copyright (i.e. that it is your own work) and that it hasn't been published previously.

If you are not comfortable about signing a contract without advice, one thing you can do is join the Society of Authors (www.societyofauthors.org). Membership is £95 per year (£68 if you are under 35) and you can become an Associate as soon as you get a book offer but are only eligible for full membership and voting rights once you have had a full-length work traditionally published, or sold over 300 print copies (500 ebook copies) of a self-published work in a 12 month period. They offer:

1. Confidential, individual contract vetting service
2. Advice about rights, fees or any other professional query you may have to help you negotiate with your publisher
3. Access to resources that will help you through the publishing process
4. Subscription to their quarterly journal, featuring articles from prominent industry professionals
5. A varied calendar of events and training sessions
6. Optional listing on their public database of members' specialisations
7. Other membership benefits

ALTERNATIVE WAYS TO GET PUBLISHED

In the old days, it was mainstream or small independent publishers or nothing. Now there is a huge choice for you. For example, you can print your own pages and have them bound by a printer, distributing them personally or through word of mouth; you can pay an online company to print 10 – 100 bound copies and continue on a print-on-demand basis so that no huge unsold stock is built up; you can pay a bit more for help with marketing, design and publicity; or you can publish your own ebook.

For ebooks, you may need some technical advice and help as you need to convert the word processed document to a digitally acceptable format. The biggest market is obviously Amazon's Kindle Store. If you would like to make your book available on the Kindle, go to Amazon's page at https://kdp.amazon.com/self-publishing/signin and follow the steps. Take care if you see adverts on the Web that offer help (at a price) to publish a Kindle book as you really shouldn't have to pay.

Whatever direction you take, you will usually need an:
- ISBN number – the 13-digit number and bar code that will uniquely mark your book and allow it to be identified and sold in bookshops. (Different rules apply for ebooks, so check with any proposed website.) You can buy this direct or use a broker, but before you pay for one, check that it is not included with any self-publishing package.
- A listing for hard copy books in the main book wholesalers' catalogues. These include Gardners and Bertram. An entire list of companies can be found at websites such as www.wholesalers365.co.uk
- Appropriate cover design and back-of-the-book blurb setting out what your book can offer readers
- Marketing strategy. This could include your own website, listings on other websites, plans to send out review copies, local events such as book signings, articles in the local press etc.

One thing not to do is sign up with the Vanity Press. These are companies that promise huge sales and marketing efforts but rarely deliver as they make their money from selling their publication service to you, NOT large numbers of books to the reading public. They will always praise your book, however badly it might be written, as all they want to do is take your money and then print your book at a high price (possibly using low quality materials), leaving it up to you to sell any copies. The trouble with these companies is that they are well-known to booksellers, and you may find it very hard to get your book into a shop if you do finally produce some hard copies.

PUBLIC LENDING RIGHT (PLR)

As soon as your book is published, it might be bought by a library. To make sure you don't lose out, you need to be aware that since 1979 the Public Lending Right Act established the right of authors to receive a small sum each time their books were borrowed from a public library.

Every year, funds provided by the Department for Culture, Media and Sport are distributed among authors, illustrators, photographers and translators according to complex calculations related to the number of books lent and the money available. For 2011/12 this amount was set at £7.4 million. Authors can earn anything from £1 to a maximum £6,600 per year.

.Distribution of these funds is managed by the PLR office based in Stockton on Tees, although the British Library has overall responsibility. The head of the PLR is known as the Registrar and you only receive funds if you register your books on their website at www.plr.uk.com or by filling in one of their forms.

Registering is easy and includes putting in personal and payment information as well as details about each book such as the publisher, year of publication, ISBN number and your role as author, co-author or other contributor.

Once you have registered your books they will only be taken into account for the current and future years as PLR cannot be earned retrospectively. Book lending data is collected from libraries annually between 1st of July and 30th of June and the fee that is arrived at, based on subsequent calculations, is made available to each author in a statement produced the following January. Payments are sent out some time in February.

Clearly, every book that is ever borrowed cannot be used in the formula and so the calculations are based on sampling actual books borrowed from a changing and anonymous group of libraries.

EXERCISE 54
1. *Go to the PLR website and, if you know you will soon be publishing a book or if you have already done so, register your details and, if relevant, register your books.*
2. *Find out the earnings of last year's top five borrowed authors, which should be listed on the site.*

****

CH. 9

WRITING FOR THE WEB AND OTHER OUTLETS

There are hundreds of books and many thousands of web pages devoted to advice on writing for the Web. Most assume that you will be working as a content writer which means that you will not only write the basic text but will also prepare the material so that it is in bite-size chunks, is easily navigable though web pages and will be found by search engines.

Although there are some features you may have to bear in mind, in many cases your text will either be published exactly as it stands or it will be reworked by someone else whose job it is to set text in code, maintain a consistent look to the pages and attract visitors to the site.

EXAMPLE

In "10 Tips for Good Web Writing," an article written by Jennifer Kyrnin, the structure of her article is exactly what you would see in a print publication, even though the instructions she provides are very different. For example, in step 2 she tells readers to: "put conclusions at the beginning", but the beginning of her own Web article is all about making sure the content is relevant to the site or page topic – no conclusions in sight. So here is an example of an article written as if for a print publication that has been put on the Web verbatim!

In my own case, I currently write a monthly computing Q & A column for www.laterlife.com, a website aimed at the Over 50s. Each month, I send in a Word document where my questions and answers are written in exactly the same way as they are when I write for a print magazine or newspaper. They may be formatted by other people in the fonts and colours used by the site but they then go online looking pretty much as they did in the original document. The main difference is that I send the images separately as jpegs and have to be careful that I identify the position in the text for these images and that the filenames I give them are appropriate to be used as captions, as that is normally where they end up. Book reviews and craft articles have also been published on the website and could equally have appeared in print.

Where my material refers readers to useful websites, I do not embed the addresses in the text in any way myself – again, this is left to technical staff.

So, when following advice you may find about writing for the Web, bear in mind that your role may be to provide copy only, rather than to format your text specially, or think about online readers and how they differ from an audience for printed copy.

EXAMPLE
I once wrote a personal account of setting up a small music club that Yours magazine was going to publish. At the last minute, the editor decided to publish another item in its place and my account was moved to their website instead. I wasn't asked to change anything and as far as I could tell, it was exactly the same piece I had sent in originally.

One place where you may well need to change your writing style is for a publisher's blog. Magazines, newspapers such as the Guardian or the Independent and other websites often publish freelance pieces to fill up their many acres of web space and they give these pages names such as Money Blog, Photography Blog etc. These are NOT the same thing as writing your own blog (which is a personal web diary where you can use any style you please). Instead they are similar to printed copy but are normally written in a more "chatty" and informal style than you would use for an article in their regular print publications.

Perhaps the best advice, as always, is to read any submission guidelines and then read a few examples of the genre produced by your prospective publisher to get an idea of the style they want. Then make sure your contribution is written in the same way.

WRITING FOR FREE

As far as the Web is concerned, you will often find there are opportunities for getting published but not necessarily for being paid for your work. Unlike writing for print publications, this is quite traditional on the Internet and there are reasons why you shouldn't automatically turn down unpaid work or insist that you are paid to start with, although you need to have some form of time limit in mind to ensure your efforts are not misused.

A few of the positive reasons for writing for free for the Web include:

- having an online presence, which can be very useful if you want to advertise your skills or be discovered as a writer (as some bloggers have found)
- using the writing as evidence for your CV or part of a writing portfolio, to lead to other writing jobs
- working for a website long enough to become an established member or contributor and eventually receive benefits including a share of revenue
- building up an expertise in the field you write about that can be as valid as working in a paid job
- allowing you time to experiment with different writing genres
- using the experience to kick-start a writing career, gaining confidence to write articles or books that stem directly from your Web experience

EXAMPLE
Julie Powell started a blog in 2002 detailing her attempts over one year to prepare all 536 recipes in Julia Child's book: "Mastering the Art of

French Cooking". Her blog was so successful that it was eventually turned into a book and a film: "Julie and Julia" starring Meryl Streep.

You can read some of the blog at

http://juliepowellbooks.com/blog.html#aug

MOST COMMON TYPES OF WORK

The Web is developing and changing all the time, but at the moment there are some basic types of writing opportunity you might find which are detailed below. To publish your writing on the Web, there are a number of different approaches you can take, for example:

- Find a specific website and contact the editor, webmaster or owner speculatively, suggesting that you write for them
- Find websites that are known to publish work from freelance writers and send in your contributions
- Apply for a specific job
- Set up your own website

EXAMPLES

Here are a few examples showing the possible range of places where online freelance writing opportunities may be available:

Websites that compliment print publications such as GP Online, the website for GP magazine

Media websites such as The Huffington Post – an American news site and blog which asks writers to write for free but where you gain status if featured

Web guides, for example Divine Coast which sets out to provide a large number of links to information on the Amalfi Coast.

Corporate websites e.g. the financial information provider SIX Financial Information

E-zines such as 'Live4ever', a music online magazine

APPROACHING WEBSITES

If you have any sort of expertise or interest in the main content of a website and feel you could write appropriate content for them, why not write and suggest they give you the opportunity? You will need to show:

- You have new ideas for articles, columns, fillers etc
- Your background is relevant and credible
- You have good writing skills
- You will be reliable and deliver on time

EXAMPLE

Some years ago, I used to write a computer queries column for a magazine called "Quicksilver" aimed at retired people, and posted answers to IT problems on the website Hairnet (later Digital Unite), which offers computer training and advice to the over 50s. After that experience, I learned that a new Over 50s website, www.laterlife.com, was starting up. I wrote to them suggesting an IT column, and have been writing for them ever since.

EXERCISE 55

1. *Return to the self-analysis you carried out for Exercise 19 and re-acquaint yourself with some of your specialist interests.*
2. *Now go online and see if you can find 4 or 5 magazine-style websites that are based around some of those topics. Make sure the website is not a personal one, as the owner will be writing all or most of the copy and so is unlikely to want to receive contributions. However, if the actual site isn't appropriate, there may be links to follow to other websites.*
3. *Look at the pages and see if you can identify a type of article or filler that you could provide.*
4. *Contact the editor and suggest a contribution that you could make.*

WHAT MATERIAL TO WRITE

The sort of jobs currently being offered for online material include article writing, forum participation, blog entries, email copy, web content, press release articles and ebooks as well as editing and proofreading work.

Blogging

This is the regular publication of opinions, advice and reviews. Blogs usually differ from mainstream articles because they are designed to allow interactions with readers by offering them a way to post their own comments on the content.

You can set up your own blog for free using a site such as www.blogger.com, or contribute pages on particular themes to sites run by others such as www.hubpages.com or www.squidoo.com. On many of the sites you will be provided with a template on which to base your blog so that it confirms to the overall style of the site.

There are various ways to earn money by writing blogs including:

- providing advertising space and earning when visitors click contextual ads that are displayed on the page (the most well known being *Google's AdSense*)
- linking to respected affiliate programs such as *Amazon* or *Skimlinks* and being paid commission to advertise products and services
- writing and selling ebooks of your own
- Sending out regular newsletters that readers subscribe to, or selling video workshops, courses etc.
- getting offers for work as an adviser or consultant, being offered speaking engagements or even gaining full-time employment once you are established as an expert in your field and have a public profile

You can also work for an organisation that will pay directly for your contributions and may also professionally edit your work before it appears. Nowadays, a growing number of media companies and public and private establishments rely on commissioning blogs from a wide range of freelance writers so that they have enough material to publish on their websites.

Article Writer

To see your own articles in print online, it is always best to set up your own website. If you aren't interested in that, a quick way is to use one of the article directories such as http://ezinearticles.com or www.buzzle.com but remember that, once an article is published, any links made elsewhere will be directed to the site rather than your own website and you may not have the rights to use the article elsewhere.

Difficult to distinguish from straight blogging sites, these article sites and others such as www.suite101.com, www.about.com, www.dorkadore.com and www.howopia.com offer browsers a wide range of written content. On some you can provide entirely your own personal choice of article or blog including recipes, opinion pieces or information, whereas others may restrict content e.g. they may mainly publish reviews or tutorials and "how to" style posts. Once again, you send in your work and if these are of a good enough standard, they are published. Earnings are normally through the volume of visitors your work attracts and the number of times adverts are clicked on the page. Eventually, regular writers may receive extra income from commissioned articles or from editing work.

Other more recognisable opportunities come from submitting articles that are more like online versions of print-style material. In most cases, you need to submit a query email as you would to a print publisher, but check the submission guidelines as sometimes, especially in the case of Web-only publishers, they may prefer to see the entire article straight away. Usually articles of this type are stand-alone, and longer or more specific in content than blog-type posts where volume and browser-attraction are their main goals.

EXERCISE 56
1. *Visit as many sites listed as you can and read some of the contributions.*
2. *If you have ideas for anything you could write, follow the guidelines and send it in.*

Content Writer

This is the main focus of courses and books on writing online content as it is writing that needs to be easily skimmed, that hooks in readers and that is designed around headings, subheadings and bullet points. It is usually linked to good quality search engine optimization (SEO) so contains keywords and strategic phrasing that enables it to be found and listed by search engines. The material has to be updated regularly so that return visitors find new and interesting content.

FINDING WORK

WARNING: it is extremely hard to find out all about an unknown company or individual advertising writing jobs online, and you will hear many stories of writers who end up sending off their work and never receiving payment, or whose rights are seriously infringed. Take great care when answering advertisements, giving bank details or signing contracts with anyone whose status cannot be verified via publicly held records.

There are still a number of genuine job opportunities for online writers and there are now a large number of vacancy websites that appear to offer freelance writing opportunities by matching writers with employers. These include www.peopleperhour.com, www.freelancer.com and www.elance.com . As well as "proper" writing jobs, there is also the chance for writers to offer "Hourlies" – skills that they sell by the hour.

EXAMPLE

One private individual providing a short-term position to writers listed this job recently: "I am looking for a talented writer to create fantastic, engaging sales copy on the listings I will be putting on eBay. I believe that fantastic sales copy will help to boost sales and give my customers a much better buying experience." This may well have been a genuine job with a credible and reliable employer, but it is hard to gauge As it was advertised on a job opportunities website, there would be some safeguards in terms of getting help from the staff there, or putting on negative feedback to warn others if there had been any bad practice.

Sadly, a common method for winning a job on these sites appears to be by underbidding everyone else, as there is rarely a fixed price and you simply have to put in the lowest amount you are prepared to work for. This means that you can be in great danger of taking on too many hours of work for a pittance. Unless you are very sure of your costs and way of working, and factor in time spent on related aspects such as research, travel or rewriting, such job websites may not be appropriate for you.

If you have the confidence and want to try, make sure you write a superb personal profile as potential employers will read these carefully, and then build up a presence on the Web that you can quote when you establish your credentials. Take care if the brief given by the employers offering writing vacancies on the freelance website are too vague or poorly worded as it may indicate a problem, such as extra hours that may have to be taken up in unexpected tasks. Good employers will make it clear exactly what they want so that you can bid for the job realistically. Established employers will also have been rated by previous freelancers, so you can see if they pay and treat their writers well.

Do not pay a website to look at job vacancies or apply. Genuine employers will find ways to advertise their vacancies and you may pay some unknown person to get a job that does not exist.

EXERCISE 57
1. *Visit some of the job websites mentioned.*
2. *Would any of the jobs be of interest to you?*

ALTERNATIVE OUTLETS

Although this book is about getting more straightforward written pieces published, it is worth bearing in mind that talented writers can also create income streams by branching off in new directions. Here are a few examples:

1. Newsletters: Set up your own website and, if you have any specialism, offer instructional or informative newsletters. Members of the public will pay you (for example through a clickable Paypal button on the site) and will then receive the newsletter on a regular basis.

2. Courses: For the more ambitious, why not offer a course? You will need to develop course materials, broken down into say 8 or 10 modules sent out each time the previous module is completed, and set up a system for students to send you assignments by email that you can mark.

3. Write courses for others: If you have a specialism, devise a course to include guidance and exercises and offer this to one of the many online or distance learning colleges around.

4. Website gateways: Many popular websites offer a central resource or a way of saving time for those interested in a particular topic such as writing competitions, understanding the tax system, buying and selling houses etc and if you can spot a gap in the market you could set up a website, create the content and perhaps make money either from advertising on the site or eventually selling your database.

5. Tutoring: Find work as a tutor for an online course provider. Students work through course material provided by the

organisation but then send you completed assignments that you mark and return.

6. Write model answers: Work for a company providing academic material e.g. model answers (NOT essays for cheats!). One company says it provides: "model essays, coursework, reports, proposals, dissertations, presentations, statistical analysis, literature reviews and personal statements."

7. Design CVs: Help people improve their CVs or covering letters. You can either work for an established company or offer this service yourself. You will clearly need to have some understanding of what is needed and perhaps design a questionnaire clients can fill in, from which you can create a draft CV to discuss with them.

EXAMPLE

One job was advertised recently worded as follows. "The brief is to write a home study course for complete beginners to social media. It should be aimed at small businesses and cover the following: Facebook, Twitter, LinkedIn, You Tube, Blogging, Strategy, Metrics and Ethics."

****

CH.10

COMPLETING THE TASK

(Many of these exercises are included in my book: "Writing Your Autobiography")

Whether you are writing a short filler, letter, article or book, it is common to find yourself feeling daunted by the hill you still have to climb.

When a writer (or anyone) faces this sort of challenge, you need to pump up the motivation and feel confident once more that you will get the job done. So here are various techniques taken from the world of life coaching that may help you.

FINDING TIME

A good avoidance tactic – certainly for some large piece of work like a whole book - is to tell yourself you don't have enough time to get down to writing. Yet most of us waste a huge amount of time that could be much better spent, including finishing a writing project.

> *EXERCISE 58*
> *To find out where you time goes, and see what minutes, hours or days you could recapture, you need to carry out the Magic Square exercise.*
>
> 1. *Draw the following labelled squares out on a piece of paper and fill in your own examples (try to find at least 5 for both NOT URGENT squares):*

See overleaf

	URGENT	NOT URGENT
IMPORTANT	Dentist appointment Catching a train Attending a meeting Taking children to school	Keeping fit e.g. going swimming Meditation Hobbies e.g. craft work, writing Seeing grandchildren
NOT IMPORTANT	Answering the phone Answering the door	Checking emails regularly Watching daytime TV Window/online shopping Going out for coffee Listening to the news every hour

2. *Now find 3 activities you could cut out of your own NOT URGENT - NOT IMPORTANT square so that you have more time for those in the shaded Magic Square, including writing.*

IDENTIFY THE BEST WAY OF WORKING

Writers use different techniques to help them complete their work, and one of these may suit you best:

- Pick a regular time each day or week to settle down to writing and stick to it. You need to know if you are a morning or evening writer so that getting up an hour earlier or staying up late may be the best way for you.

- Plan out periods when you know you can work undisturbed and keep to a definite timetable
- Try to write something for five minutes every day, whether you want to or not. You will usually find that you then change your mind and want to continue.
- Work on a more ad hoc basis, as and when ideas come to you, if this has proved in the past to be the right way for you to work. Monitor yourself carefully in case it turns out to be an excuse not to write.

EXERCISE 59

1. *Over the next few days, write down where and when you are writing.*
2. *If there is a pattern, see if you can come up with a schedule or rules to follow to optimise your writing effectiveness.*

WRITER'S BLOCK

There may be times when the whole task you've set yourself or at least one part of it seems too much, and you find yourself sitting looking at a blank piece of paper without any idea of what to put down. This is a well-known phenomenon known as writer's block.

If you worry it may happen to you or you have experienced it in the past, here are a few possible remedies:

- Establish a routine and stick to it. It is often easier to write when you have to rather than wait until you feel like it.
- Set realistic targets. Don't expect to write five pages a day, but set as a target something sensible and achievable like two paragraphs. When you've written that you may well

feel like writing some more. (See SMART goal setting below for more ideas).

- Leave off in mid-flow rather than finishing a section or scene neatly, so that you won't have to start all over again next time. When you sit down to finish off the piece you left, you may find you get into a writing rhythm and have the energy to carry on to the next section.

- Impose a deadline. If you tell yourself you must finish a particular section or cover a certain subject by the end of the day, it may motivate you to keep writing.

- Start a diary or just write anything for five minutes. With no pressure to write well, just noting down what you did yesterday or making a shopping list may get you back into writing mode.

- Do something constructive that is not this particular piece of writing. If you really cannot face the page, read a reference book on your subject, sort through some of your resources, go to the library or complete some of the exercises in this book that you may have skipped e.g. fill in an extra bit of your time line. Taking your mind off the task for a while may be just what you need.

SMART GOAL SETTING

It is easier to complete a task if you have an obvious target to aim at, and one technique common in the business world is SMART Goal Setting. When a large task appears so huge that you cannot face it, you often resort to avoidance tactics. On the other hand, you can usually manage a single step forward. SMART goal setting involves identifying and then taking a series of small steps, one at a time, until you realise you have reached your ultimate goal.

Imagine you want to write an article about learning French. For each step:

S stands for specific. This means you must set a very specific target. Instead of the vague idea of "talking to everyone who taught me

French", a specific goal might be to phone up Susan Smith and arrange to have a chat about primary school French lessons.

M stands for measurable. Here you must set a target that can be measured e.g. in time, distance, number of pages written, boxes sorted or some other factor. So instead of phoning Susan to arrange to meet in a general sense, you goal could be to arrange to talk to Susan for an hour when she is free.

A stands for achievable. If Susan lives abroad or many miles away, arranging a meeting will be impossible for a while. So here your goal should be to arrange a time you can talk over the phone for an hour.

R stands for realistic. It won't work if you are overambitious and try the impossible. So if you have no idea where Susan Smith lives or what her phone number might be, you need to find someone else like Steven to talk to whilst trying to get hold of Susan's contact details.

T stands for time sensitive. Here you need to set a date or time by which you will achieve your goal. In our example, you could decide that you will have had the chat with Susan or Steven by the end of next week.

Whether you have achieved this first SMART goal or missed your deadline, you need to review progress. There are now two possible actions:

- Rewrite the goal (if it was too ambitious or other circumstances got in the way)
- Move on to the next step and set a new SMART goal e.g. based on the discussion to write two pages about learning French by Thursday.

EXERCISE 60

    1. Finish the sentence: "My SMART goal is to
      ....
      .... "

    2. Set about achieving it.

> 3. *When the time limit is reached, review the goal and either set a new one or rewrite it and attempt to achieve this newly worded goal instead.*

USE AFFIRMATIONS TO KEEP MOTIVATED

The subconscious is very strong and if you have in-built feelings that you are a failure or you have no confidence in your abilities, these thoughts will keep emerging and will sabotage your efforts. One way to change your way of thinking is a technique known as Affirmations.

This technique is not for everyone but there is some truth in the idea that, if you say something enough times you start to believe it and it becomes self-fulfilling. So if you tell yourself (affirm) that you will complete your article or book, there is more chance that this will turn out to be true.

For an affirmation to work properly, as you may be attempting the difficult task of changing your personal beliefs, it needs to be set up in the following way.

1. Decide on the topic. In our case it will be related to completing your article or book, but it could be general e.g. become more self-confident or to enjoy life more.

2. Imagine what it will be like if you are successful. Create a picture in your mind of how you will feel when your book has been written and published. See people responding to a copy, and imagine the book on the shelf in a bookshop.

3. Write your affirmation in the following format:
   a. In the first person
   b. In the present
   c. The wording must make you feel excited.

For example: *I am a great writer and people love reading my book.*

4. Repeat your affirmation many times a day and, as you do so, run through the images you created in your mind when you imagined succeeding.

5. Say it out loud and, if you feel like it, share it with other people.

6. Remind yourself of the affirmation. Try writing it on small pieces of paper, or use pictures that summon it up, and leave these around where you will keep seeing them.

EXERCISE 61

Write out an appropriate affirmation and have a go at repeating it, especially just before you go to sleep.

APPENDIX 1

Here are a few books that I have found helpful when writing non-fiction, as well as one book of my own:

"Writing Successful Self-help and How-to Books" by Jean Marie Stine, published by John Wiley & Sons

"The Serious Guide to Joke Writing" by Sally Holloway, published by www.bookshaker.com

"Writing Your Autobiography" by Jackie Sherman, published by Emerald Publishing

APPENDIX 2

ANSWER TO EXERCISE 33

After holidaying in Barcelona, we left our hotel to get to the airport several hours early, to leave time for lunch and some final shopping. Our hotel had been picked for its location so all we had to do was wheel our cases round the corner and catch one of the frequent airport buses.

Bag checks done, boarding passes in hand, we found ourselves on a mezzanine floor, overlooking a large shopping mall. Down below, restaurants, shops and coffee bars where spread out before us and our main problem would be deciding where to eat. Above our heads was a large notice with an arrow pointing to our boarding gate and nothing else visible except an unmarked escalator, a scrolling advertising screen and the passport checkpoint manned by a smiling officer. Passport checks took a few seconds and we were now through, ready to make our way down to the treasures below.

We wandered along the concourse both left and right, but could only find one down escalator clearly marked "Toilets Only". So we stopped a passing stewardess to ask her how to reach the shops.

"You have passed passport control," she said, and made to walk off. I stopped her with a light hand on her sleeve.
"Yes, that's right. So how do we get to the shops?"
"No," she said severely. "You have come through passport control. You cannot go there." And this time I let her go.

Non comprendo, I thought to myself, although her English was perfect. There was clearly a communication problem so we found a cleaner. His English was poor, but understandable.
"You come through here. You cannot go there."

Finally, in the small gift shop, I was given a fuller explanation.
"Didn't you see the notice?" asked the saleswoman.

"What notice?"

Just then, we heard an English voice asking someone in the shop how they could get downstairs to the restaurants. So we weren't the only idiot tourists to miss this large notice.

"The large green notice by passport control. It says once you have your passport checked you cannot return."

Well, excuse me but there was no notice. Just a scrolling advertising board we hardly glanced at. Was that it?